SPIRITUAL SONGS V:

DAWN THROUGH DUSK

I0150616

"Hands held up together toward the Heavenly skies, I pray for all humans around the globe from dawn through dusk."

Ann Marie Ruby

Copyright © 2026 Ann Marie Ruby

All rights reserved. No part of this book may be reproduced in any
form or stored in any retrieval system without prior written permission
from the publisher. Book cover images are composed of stock photos
from shutterstock.com, and/or specifically illustrated for this book.
Interior images are composed of stock photos from shutterstock.com,
and/or specifically illustrated for this book.

Disclaimer:

This book ("*Spiritual Songs V: Dawn Through Dusk*") only
represents the personal views of the author. In no way, does it represent
or endorse any religious, philosophical, political, or scientific view. It
has been written in good faith for people of all cultures and beliefs.
Any resemblance to actual persons, living or dead, is purely
coincidental.

Published in the United States of America, 2026.

ISBN-13: 979-8-9917416-8-2

DEDICATION

"Day breaks as the glorious Sun shines upon all creation of the one Creator, guiding and reminding them dusk will soon be upon them, so not to leave behind hope, faith, and belief."

ANN MARIE RUBY

Travelers travel the lonely path of obstacles trying to find a job, trying to pay off debt, praying to be healed, and trying to overcome all other obstacles throughout the day. The obstacles travel with them even when they try to transition from dawn to dusk and want to rest their tired souls. I want you to know whatever bridge of obstacles you are on, your Creator is there holding on to your hands at all times. All you need to do to find Him is hold on to your faith.

Know there is always a prayer which is a staircase or a bridge that will connect you the creation to your Creator as we all come from God, and we shall go back to God. In between we have the journey through life. Live in peace and spread peace. Live with one another, not against for in union we are all the creation of the one Creator.

I dedicate this book to all looking for strength, guidance, and help through their journey of life as we are all the one creation of the one Creator.

TABLE OF CONTENTS

INTRODUCTION

"The one creation
Of the one Creator
Of the one world,
We are not divided
But united.
For the Creator,
As the creation
From dawn through dusk
We recite in union,
Spiritual Songs."

Evolution from dawn to dusk is when we the humans transition from light to dark. We travel from the glowing sunlight to the reflection of the Sun's glow, when we cannot see everything, nor do we know what lies ahead of us. Yet we all know as dusk comes upon us, dawn too will break open soon. During this time, we the humans connect to our Creator and ask, seek, and knock upon the doors of divine intervention.

It is a time for the humans to not lose hope, but renew their hope, faith, and belief, and reconnect with the Divine. Believe in the miracles of dawn as dawn will break open after the darkness fades. Know this and believe in divine intervention. Walk through the dark night with a prayer in your hand. Watch how our Creator ends the darkness with the brightest star we can see. The Sun comes and kisses us at the first sight of dawn.

With faith in knowing that dawn will come again, walk through all the darkness within your life with a smile on your face. Pain, loss, and sufferings come and greet all of us at different corners of life. We do not get to choose the obstacles of life as they come uninvited and enter our lives even through the closed doors. At that specific moment, I want all of you to remember how darkness evaporates at dawn. Just like that, your specific obstacle too will end at the first glimpse of your life's dawn. Yes, I can hear you ask, but how long do I have to suffer?

Time and tide are something we the humans cannot control. Yet I know our Creator will answer and provide for us at His time, not ours. So, we ask, knock, and seek, and then we wait. While we have within our control the patience of waiting, the Creator has all the answers. Maybe not all the answers are the ones we want to hear, but at the end, only our Creator knows what is good or what is bad for us. The daylight hours seem so long as the night seems longer when we are covered by the blankets of obstacles.

I want all of you during this time of the darkness to carry within your hands the candles of hope. The prayers I have written with blessed words are my candles of hope for all of you. I call this book *Spiritual Songs V: Dawn Through Dusk*. Open any one of the pages and recite these prayers I call songs. They will give you, the individual, the strength needed to keep on going. At all times, remember, there is another person in this world who is going through what you are going through. Some have walked out of this hurdle before you, but you too will overcome this hurdle. The suffering is hard and the time waiting for this suffering to pass is even harder.

Just hold on to the prayers on these pages and believe the miracles of dawn will arrive within your corner too. I know dusk is a sign the day will end soon. But remember after dusk, there is only one way out, and that is dawn. You will travel to dawn after your balance between day and night is figured out. The veil that covers the known and unknown is frightening but will be uncovered through the tides of time. Carry within your soul, during this time, your faith, belief, and hope.

Never lose hope as hope never gives up on you. For you, the individual walking through the hardest period of your life, I have written these prayers I call songs. Each prayer is a reminder that a new dawn is a new beginning. A new day is waiting for you at the end of the night. Call upon your Creator and know He is there calling upon you too for the love between a creation and the Creator is what these prayers are written through and from.

Today, you too have them within your hands. Believe in yourself and your Creator, and know these words are just words that will help your inner soul to reconnect with the Creator. As your day ends within obstacles or blessings, remember to watch the sunset as after the Sun sets, a new dawn will shine upon you. There and then, you will have another chance to remove all your obstacles. Take today as a blessing. Your prayers will be answered as long as you believe and keep praying without giving up on hope, faith, and belief.

I have named this book *Dawn Through Dusk* as I believe we try to overcome all the hurdles before darkness envelopes our horizon. We try to hold on to the last light of the day and then the obstacles just overburden us. Holding on to the blanket of hope, faith, and belief, we will cross the darkness to get back over to the light of dawn. Our Creator who created dawn and dusk will guide us through everything as He holds our hands and walks with us. We will feel His hold only when we believe.

I crossed the obstacles after climbing over the hurdles all day and staying awake all night. Realizing twilight hours were finally upon me, I wrote for you and for me my book of hope. I, a creation, of the Most Loving, Most Kind, Most Merciful, the Creator, have called upon Him through my words I call songs. Today for all of you the creation of the one Creator of the one world, I have woven 101 prayer songs for 101 days into a book I call *Spiritual Songs V: Dawn Through Dusk.*

PRAYERS:

Dawn Through Dusk

A BLESSED NEW DAWN

Oh my God, the Omnipotent,

As dawn appears before us today,

I pray for good health,

Good wealth,

And good luck.

Oh my God,

I pray for safety,

Guidance,

And wisdom.

Oh my God,

As I break bread,

I pray may all my mistakes

Be forgiven as I repent,

Redeem,

And awaken

Through the knowledge

That after dusk,

After darkness,

My God, my Creator,

Always bestows upon all His creation

A BLESSED NEW DAWN.

So Be It

A CLOUDY, FOGGY, OR SUNNY DAWN

My Lord,

The Omnipotent,

Dawn broke open

As we were greeted

With a foggy and cloudy day.

As the clouds and fog disappear,

I know

Miracles in life

Too start to appear.

I pray with all

My heart,

My mind,

My body,

And my soul

To place an umbrella of protection

Made from my prayers

Over

My beloved ones.

May they all

Be safe,

Be healthy,

Be wealthy,

Be happy,

And always

Be Your blessed creation.

May they always remember to pray

And never forget

The one God,

The one Creator,

The Omnipotent,

And remember

Through all cloudy

And all sunny days,

We must never forget to pray.

Through prayers,

All the clouds and the fog disappear.

A prayer recited from

A creation's inner soul

Reaches

The one Creator,

The one God,

The Omnipotent,

As He answers all prayers recited

Through

A CLOUDY, FOGGY, OR SUNNY DAWN.

So Be It

ACCEPT MY PRAYER AT DAWN

On this blissful day,

I pray to You my Lord

For calmness,

For peace,

And for joy to come

And stay within my soul.

May I be blessed with

Good health,

Great wealth,

Prosperity,

Love,

And happiness.

My Lord,

Take away

All the obstacles,

All the hurdles,

All the challenges,

And all the negativities

From my life.

Oh my Lord,

Accept my repentance

As I have repented

For all my known,

And unknown sins.

May my prayers

Filled with words of repentance

Remove all my sins.

May these blessed words

Wash away

All the negativities

From my mind,

My body,

And my soul.

May all humans who

Recite this prayer be forgiven

If and only when they

Repent,

Redeem,

And awaken

With their innermost hearts

Filled with love for You,

My Lord,

And with complete faith

In the power of the Omnipotent,

The Omnipresent,

And the Omniscient.

My Lord,

The Creator

Of all humans,

Animals,

Spirits,

Angels,

Heavens above, Earth beneath,

And the whole celestial world,

Today, accept my prayer.

Grant me one wish,

I ask, seek,

And have been knocking for.

Oh my Lord,

The Merciful,

The Giver of everything,

Grant me this one wish

I have been knocking

On Your door for.

Grant me my wish that I have

In my innocent mind sought

And asked You for.

My Lord, my Creator,

ACCEPT MY PRAYER AT DAWN.

So Be It

ALLURE OF DAWN

My God,

The Omnipotent,

As dreariness engulfs

All around me,

I pray to You,

My God,

My Creator,

To see,

To hear,

And to talk for me.

I fear the

Hateful verses

Of the gossipers

And the whisperers.

They are blanketed

With immoral and unjust

Anger,

Revenge,

And division,

Created by the ones

Who fear not anything.

They are full of

Pride,

Envy,

Gluttony,

Greed,

Lust,

Sloth,

And become

A wrath

For all devotees

Who wish to avoid all deadly sins,

Who wish to remain pure and clean.

Oh my God,

As the world turns dark,

And the retributive souls

Travel within groups,

Trying to convert

And carry all innocent souls

To the dark path,

I, Your devoted creation,

Raise my hands in prayer.

With the power

Of my blessed prayer,

I knock,

Seek,

And ask for

Your protection,

Your intervention,

And Your guidance

To carry me

Out of the sinful waters

Of the dark times.

My prayers become

My saving grace

Like the miraculous lotus

Which will carry me

Out of the dark times.

With my faith and hope

Completely intact,

My prayers

Will burn

All forbidden sins

And will remove

All the wrongful convictions

Of the wrong

As I pray and witness

The glowing

ALLURE OF DAWN.

So Be It

ANOTHER BLESSED DAWN

I pray to my God,

The Omnipotent,

On this blessed day

As dawn broke open

And evaporated the darkness,

May we, Your creation,

Be blessed with wisdom,

Financial support,

And job security.

As this world

Is home to all

Obstacles,

Dangers,

And challenges,

May we the precants,

Not get lost,

Not be scared,

And not be amongst

The cursed,

But be amongst

The blessed,

The favored,

And the saved.

May we be amongst

The ones

Who have repented,

Not the ones

Who have gone astray.

Oh my God,

My Creator,

The Alpha,

And the Omega,

May I, Your devotee,

Be blessed

And be protected

Within Your embrace.

I know

You bless this world

And all Your creation,

The found

And the lost,

With another chance

In life

As You gift all

ANOTHER BLESSED DAWN.

So Be It

ANOTHER NEW DAWN

I pray to my Lord,

On this blessed day,

As dawn peeks through

My windows,

And gifts

A beautiful day,

May we Your creation

Always have on our plates,

Good health, wealth, and wisdom.

May we be safe,

Protected,

And obstacle free.

May all of Your creation

On this Earth,

Wake up with a smile

And go to bed

With a smile,

And wait with

A smile on their

Faces for

ANOTHER NEW DAWN.

So Be It

ANOTHER SACRED DAWN

My God, the Omnipotent,

From the first break of dawn,

May my first breath

Take only Your name.

With the first sight of dawn,

I give my morning grace.

Oh my God,

Bless us,

Your creation,

As we break the first slice of bread.

With this bread in my hands,

I pray may we, Your creation,

Always have food

On our plates,

And a roof

Over our head.

My God, the Omnipotent,

Protect us throughout the day.

May we be safe, healthy, happy,

And financially stable.

Oh my God,

As the day turns to dusk,

May we return home,

Safe and secure,

To our families,

Who wait

With bread

On their plates

To share with all.

As we unitedly recite

Our blessed sunset prayer

To be safe throughout

The dark nights,

Oh my God,

Bless our families,

And those who

Have no family

To go home to,

May they have a family

To go home to,

So, we Your creation

Have someone in our lives,

And a safe dwelling

To return to,

And enough bread

To share with all.

SPIRITUAL SONGS V: DAWN THROUGH DUSK

Oh my God,

With my family

I pray may You,

The Omnipotent,

Bless us with grace,

Honor,

And dignity,

So we do not go astray,

Or fall prey,

Through the

Dark nights.

May Your stars,

And Your blessed

Glowing Moon

Guide us

To the right path,

The path

You have laid out

For us,

Not the path

That has

Not been blessed

By You.

Oh my God, the Omnipotent,

I pray to You throughout

The dark nights

To protect

And take me,

And my family

To yet

Another blessed day.

May we have yet

Another chance,

And another opportunity

To witness

The first amber glow

Of Your blessed Sun

Which shall come

Again

After the dark night's struggles.

I awaken

And witness,

Yet again,

Through

My God's

Blessings,

ANOTHER SACRED DAWN.

So Be It

ANOTHER SANCTIFIED DAWN

I pray on this blessed day,

May we have

Health,

Wealth,

And wisdom.

May we not go astray

Or forget the commandments

Given by our God,

The Omnipotent,

To keep us safe,

So, we never get lost

During the struggles of life.

Oh my God, my Creator,

The Omnipotent,

The Omnipresent,

The Omniscient,

Hold our hands.

Guide us

To the right path

That has been

Blessed by You.

Oh my God,

ANN MARIE RUBY

As dawn breaks open,

And we, Your creation,

Walk through our life,

May we always have

Your blessed hands

Guiding and blessing us.

Each day and

Each night,

We are blessed

To be able to break bread

With Your blessings.

Through the day,

And through the night,

Then my God,

With all the learned lessons,

And with the daily prayer of

Repentance,

Redemption,

And awakening from within

Our inner soul,

We again

Witness

ANOTHER SANCTIFIED DAWN.

So Be It

APPEARANCE OF DAWN

Oh my God,

As I wake up

And say my prayers,

I remember all my troubles.

I never give up on hope,

On faith,

Or on belief

Through all the troubles of life

As I know my God is there.

When I fall,

I get up again as I know

My God holds my hands.

When I cry,

I know my God is there

With His hands

Catching my tears.

So, I pray and I say

Never shall I

Give up on hope.

When everything seems wrong,

I still pray as I say,

Never shall I

Give up on faith,

For I believe

All the dark clouds will fade.

When darkness comes,

I still pray for I know

Never shall I

Stop believing my God is there

For my God

Has never left me.

I, Your creation,

With my belief,

With my faith,

And with my hope,

Keep praying.

Like a miracle,

After crossing

All the bridges of obstacles,

I see my God smiles

As all the darkness disappears.

The Sun shines upon me as

I witness

The

APPEARANCE OF DAWN.

So Be It

AT ANOTHER AUSPICIOUS DAWN

I pray on this blessed day,

To receive from my Lord,

Glad tidings, mercy, and blessings

On this beautiful day.

I pray on this blessed day,

To be able to share with this world,

Kindness, compassion, and smiles

On this miraculous day.

I pray on this blessed day,

To be always grateful and thankful

For all the things received

On this merciful day.

I pray on this blessed day,

To be able to pray on my knees as nightfall approaches,

And to be able to greet

Another marvelous day.

I pray on this blessed day,

To be able to hear my Lord

With kindness, compassion, and smiles,

As He says to have a wonderful day

AT ANOTHER AUSPICIOUS DAWN.

So Be It

AT DAWN

The lonely traveler I am

Who lives on Earth,

Scared of life,

Scared of the others,

Scared of the outcomes,

Scared of financial burdens,

Scared of failures,

Scared of deadly diseases,

Scared of anger,

Scared of being wrong,

Scared to say something,

And scared not to say something.

Oh my God,

The journey seems long, dark, and scary

As I wait here on the lonely path

For guidance from

You, my God, my Creator

To erase all my fears

All my worries,

And all my troubles

AT DAWN.

So Be It

AT THE MIRACULOUS GLIMPSE OF DAWN

As dawn smiled upon us,

May I, Your creation,

Not be overcome

By the distractions of life.

I prayed all night

My God, my Creator,

For dawn to smile

Upon me.

I prayed all night

For You, my God,

To lift all

My obstacles,

And bless me

Away from all darkness.

Yet as I stand during

The daylight hours,

You blessed me

And removed

Darkness away

From my life.

I pray

May I not go astray,

Or fall prey with

The seven deadly sins.

My God, my Creator,

May I, Your creation,

Not fall prey to

Pride,

Envy,

Gluttony,

Greed,

Lust,

Sloth,

Or wrath.

May I remember

My sufferings,

And my struggles

From dusk to dawn,

And may I

Always have faith

And hope,

To carry me,

Over the obstacles

Of life.

Oh my God, my Creator,

May my mind, body, and soul

Always be pure and clean.

May the lessons

Of the dark night's struggles

Always remind me

To be a human,

A devotee

Whom my God, my Creator,

Can call His

Blessed creation,

Who never went astray

Even when

The Moon

Appeared on Earth,

And the fallen stars

Spread

Tempting temptations

Till the embers of

The amazing Sun

Burned all temptations,

All sins,

And all the

Forbidden paths

AT THE MIRACULOUS GLIMPSE OF DAWN.

So Be It

AWAKEN THROUGH THE LIGHT OF DAWN

Lost and asleep

Within all the darkness,

Are all the lost souls,

All the troubled travelers,

And all the wrongful voices of the wrong.

They are positive

And guarantee

Their ways,

Their words,

And their beliefs are

The only way,

Only path,

And only guide.

My mind says,

No.

My body says,

No.

My soul says,

No.

My mind,

My body,

And my soul

Say

There are

Not different paths.

There are not different ways

Or different routes.

If the destination

Is the same,

My mind,

My body,

And my soul

Say there is one Creator.

We are all

The creation

Who shall realize

And know

This sacred

And

Blessed truth

As we all

Eventually

After the struggles

Through the darkness

AWAKEN THROUGH THE LIGHT OF DAWN.

So Be It

BATTLES END AT DAWN

The storms are brewing
All over,
All around,
All above,
And all under me.
Oh my God,
The Omnipotent,
The Remover of all obstacles,
Help me and guide me out
From all the storms of life.
Save me my God
From getting lost through
The obstacles of life.
May I be strong.
May I be energetic.
May I not fall from grace.
May I not go astray.
As the hurdles come
And declare a war
Between my faith and my belief,
May I not be placed
On the dark streets of the lost

Minds,

Bodies,

And souls.

Oh my God,

I pray through

The struggles of life,

Financial burdens,

And family and marital troubles,

May, I, Your creation,

Not fall prey and lose

My connection to You.

Throughout all the darkness,

I believe and know

My God will never let me go

As this is only a test.

I know with faith

And complete belief,

The Sun shall shine

After the dark times.

The Sun's rays

Shall come pouring through

To say all

BATTLES END AT DAWN.

So Be It

BE HEALTHY AT DAWN

Human voices cry

As the bodies tremble in pain.

The minds become murky.

The souls become bewildered.

Oh my God,

Your humans engulfed in sickness

Ask, seek, and knock on Your gate

For an interception,

For an intercession,

For an intermediary.

Oh my God,

The Omnipotent,

The Omnipresent,

The Omniscient,

Open the gates of healing

As we recite this blessed prayer

From our mind,

Our body,

And our soul

To

BE HEALTHY AT DAWN.

So Be It

BE IT DAWN OR BE IT DUSK

When the skies smile,

Pouring the first

Rays of light,

I pray.

As the day

Becomes hot

And uncomfortable,

I pray.

Drenched in

Freezing cold,

Pouring rain,

I never lose my faith

As I pray.

When the troubles

Pour down upon me,

Like a glass of ice,

When pain, fear, and troubles

Refuse to fade away

Like the floating clouds,

I still pray.

As I am pulled

Toward hope,

And toward the promises,

My inner mind,

My body,

And my soul

Believe and know

My guiding light

Is always there.

Behind all the clouds,

All the difficult times,

I know my faith,

My belief,

And my love

Will call upon my God,

The Omnipotent,

As I know

He is always near.

I never fear

As all the troubles are nothing

For I have as my shield

Against all the troubles of life,

My prayers.

So, let me pray

BE IT DAWN OR BE IT DUSK.

So Be It

BLESS MY DAWN PRAYERS

My Lord,

The fog-covered morning

Glances back at me

Through the windows,

Yet I know the fog will disappear

And the glorious Sun

Will shine through

My windows.

With this belief and faith,

I know even in my life,

The fog will evaporate.

I know I will be

At the destination

You will me to be.

May I, my Lord,

Through this belief and faith

Have the financial sustenance

To live on Earth

With dignity and honor.

My Lord,

Bless me and bless my family

With good health and prosperity.

My Lord,

May all obstacles

Be removed

From my life

And the lives of my family.

May I be blessed with

Love, honor, and justice on Earth.

My Lord,

Remove all the obstacles

And allow me

To have a blessed life on Earth.

My Lord,

I pray You accept my prayers.

Accept my prayers, my Lord,

Accept my prayers, my Lord

For I only ask, seek, and knock

Upon Your door.

As I open my eyes

First thing this morning,

These are my dawn prayers

That will last eternally.

Oh my Lord,

BLESS MY DAWN PRAYERS.

So Be It

BLESSED BE THROUGH DUSK THROUGH DAWN

Where there are obstacles,

I pray to my God

As He says, "Remove all obstacles."

I say, "Blessed be!"

When I fall into financial hurdles,

I pray to my God

As He says, "Remove all financial hurdles."

I say, "Blessed be!"

As I get into health crises,

I pray to my God

As He says, "Remove all health crises."

I say, "Blessed be!"

As I fall into darkness,

I pray to my God

As He says, "Let there be dawn."

Through all obstacles,

All financial burdens,

All health crises,

I say, "Blessed be. Blessed be. Blessed be.

BLESSED BE THROUGH DUSK THROUGH DAWN."

So Be It

BLESSED DAWN

My God,

My Creator,

I pray

On this blessed day,

May we,

Your true devotees,

Your blessed creation,

All find in our fate,

Good health,

Good wealth,

And good luck.

My God,

My Creator,

I pray,

May we, Your creation,

With these blessings,

Never lose hope

And never fall prey.

May we never forget

When and where

All seem dark,

All seem lost,

And nothing adds up,

It is then,

We, the creation,

Must stop,

Let go of all the worries

And all the fear,

And remember to pray.

For in life or in death

We, Your creation,

My God,

My Creator,

Eternally need

The support

Of Your blessed hands,

The hands of

The Creator,

The Omnipotent,

To hold us,

The creation,

To stand

And walk

Into the

BLESSED DAWN.

So Be It

BLESSED GUIDANCE OF DAWN

My God, my Creator,

The Creator of all creations,

The Creator of Earth,

Heavens above,

And all existence,

Some of Your

Self-proclaimed

Powerful humans on Earth

Are giving wrong directions.

They are taking

Your creation,

The humans,

On the boat of the ones

Who have gone astray.

With powerful voices of the wrong,

With sweet tempting ways,

They take Your creation

On their sinful boat

That drowns and washes away

All of Your commandments,

My God, my Creator.

I pray on this dark night,

May I not be upon that boat.

May I not fall

Into the world of the astray,

Or fall prey

To the tempting words and ways.

I pray

My God,

Guide me always.

May my mind,

My body,

And my soul,

Never fall to temptations.

May I be protected from all sins,

And all the powerful actions

Of the wrong,

Even though they make them right

On Earth by their rule of law.

They go against Your laws,

Your commandments,

And Your given guidance.

May I have the courage,

The wisdom,

And the strength

To simply say,

No

To my friends,

To my family,

And to my society

When I must.

I pray my God,

Guide me throughout

My time on Earth.

May I only board

The boat

Of the Omnipotent

As all the obscurity

Disappears.

The wrong and the right

Can be visible

To all eyes

When the biggest star

Appears

With messages from

The Omnipotent,

The Omnipresence,

As

BLESSED GUIDANCE OF DAWN.

So Be It

BLESSINGS OF LOVE AT DAWN

Oh my God,

I pray to You,

The Remover of

All obstacles.

On this dark

And mysterious

Morning,

I ask You,

My God, my Creator,

To remove all my obstacles.

Oh my God,

Remove all my physical

And emotional pain

For it is hard at times

To even pray when

All the pain takes over

This earthly body.

Oh my God,

Remove all my financial burdens

For this world revolves

Around financial needs.

Oh my God,

On every path I take,

There is a hurdle.

I ask You,

My God, my Creator,

The Remover of

All hurdles,

Please with this prayer,

Remove all

The hurdles

Of my life.

My God, my Creator,

You have blessed

All Your creation

With true love

And harmony.

I pray as the darkness disappears,

I too have as Your blessing,

True love

And harmony

As I see Your Sun breaking through

And bringing forth

Into my life,

BLESSINGS OF LOVE AT DAWN.

So Be It

BLESSINGS POUR AT DAWN

The Sun breaks through

As it dawns upon us,

It is a wonderful day.

Oh my God,

On this bright, fun, and blessed day,

I give my grace.

As I break my bread

And I take my first steps outside,

I give my grace.

What a wonderful life

As I meet

And greet Your creation.

As I return home to my family

And break bread again,

Oh my God,

Thank You

For another miraculous sunset.

As I go to bed,

I say blessed be, blessed be, blessed be.

Let my God's

BLESSINGS POUR AT DAWN.

So Be It

BREAK OF DAWN

My God,

Accept

My calls.

Accept

My asking,

My seeking,

And my knocking

As I knock upon Your doors

For good health.

My God,

Show us

Where we are

To be

And how we are

To travel

In life.

Oh my God,

Place us

Upon the path

You have created for us.

Give us the sustenance

To live life

On Your blessed Earth

With honor,

Dignity,

And courage,

With good health,

Wealth,

And sustenance.

My God,

Bestow mercy upon us.

My God,

Accept our repentance

And answer our prayers

As we, Your creation,

Pray at the

First sight of dawn.

May my dawn prayer

On this day be accepted

By my God,

My Creator,

As I pray

For my family

At the first

BREAK OF DAWN.

So Be It

BREAK OPEN DAWN

My Lord,

The Omnipotent,

At dawn,

I pray to You

For Your children.

May they always have

Your mercy,

Blessings,

Grace,

And forgiveness.

May You,

My God, my Creator,

Always protect,

Preserve,

And keep them safe.

Oh my God,

Always in life,

Let my pure praying soul

Through my blessed prayers

Be there with Your children.

As a guide

And a protector,

SPIRITUAL SONGS V: DAWN THROUGH DUSK

I know

Prayers recited for

Your children

Never go lost,

Never go forgotten,

And never go away.

So, today as the dark night

Has faded away,

And the glorious Sun welcomed all,

I pray for Your children,

Oh my God, my Creator,

Through Your

Divine blessings.

Let my prayers

Break open the darkness,

And may this

Innocent soul's

Cries and calls

Be known as

The miracle of a

Creation's blessings,

That

BREAK OPEN DAWN.

So Be It

BRIDGE OF FAITH AT DAWN

Oh my God, my Creator,

I kneel on my knees

And bow my head down

As I, Your beloved creation,

Pray for faith.

My God,

The Most Kind,

I stand in front of You

With all my obstacles,

And with all physical

And emotional pain.

I stand with

All my financial difficulties

As I feel lost.

I feel lonely as I am left

Alone and stranded.

I only pray to You,

My God the Merciful,

To guide me

To You.

For with the obstacles

And all the troubles

Over the path of my life,

May I not go astray

Or fall prey

To disappointment,

Depression,

And anger.

May I not through

The troubles of life,

Get distanced from You,

My God,

The Most Loving.

I pray with all my being,

With all my heart,

And with all my belief,

May I through everything

Find the glimmer of hope

That will

Hold me steady

On the bridge of faith.

Oh my God,

The Most Forgiving,

I pray,

You forgive me,

And send to me,

From the beyond,

Messages of

Hope,

Faith,

And

Love.

Give me strength, courage,

And tolerance

Through life.

Oh my God,

May my faith

Never wilt,

Never break,

Or never let me down.

I know I will,

Always through

All the obstacles

And all the blessings,

From dawn,

Through dusk,

Through dawn,

Pray to You.

May my love for You

Never cease

As I know

My God's love for me

And my love for my God,

Through faith,

Keeps me in

A bond eternally.

Oh my God,

The Omnipotent,

I pray to You

To uphold my faith,

My heart,

And my spirit.

Allow all the troubles

In my life

To be resolved

Through my faith

As where there is faith,

There is the bridge

Over the troubles of life.

I know my God,

The Omnipresence,

Is found

Everywhere,

Within the

Troubling times,

And within the

Joyful events.

So today,

I pray

To You,

My God,

The Omniscient,

To never let me go.

From dawn

Through dusk,

Through dawn,

Hold on to me,

As I

Hold on to my faith

And pray.

As I witness,

The first glimpse of light

Gleaming through the clouds

Onto the Earth,

May I eternally stand upon

The

BRIDGE OF FAITH AT DAWN.

So Be It

CALL OF DAWN

Oh my God,

My Creator,

As dawn

Beckons me,

I open my eyes

And I know

I must sit up

And pray.

All the troubles,

All the fear,

And all the pain

I suffer

And go through

Is nothing

Compared to

My faith,

My belief,

And my hope

That my God,

The Omnipotent,

Has brought upon me

A new dawn

And a new day.

I was able to

Walk across

The dark night's

Bridge of struggles

With

My faith,

My belief,

And complete hope

That I will be fine

As my God,

The Alpha

And the Omega,

Is always there.

Will all my faith

And my hope,

I believe

My God

Has sent me

The first sign of proof

That my beacon of hope

Is the

CALL OF DAWN.

So Be It

CHOOSE TO FORGIVE FROM DAWN

Mercy

I seek from

You,

Oh my God,

My Creator,

As I choose

To be merciful

Toward all Your creation.

Oh my God,

My Creator,

I release all from debt

As I want

To be debt-free.

Oh my God,

My Creator,

I choose to love

Over all anger

As I call upon You,

The Most Kind

And the Most Loving.

Oh my God,

My Creator,

I pardon all

Who wronged me

As I ask You

To pardon me

For all my wrong.

Oh my God,

My Creator,

I choose to live

Life on the path

Where I see

All Your blessed and forgiven

Creation walk.

Oh my God,

My Creator,

With this prayer,

May I be forgiven

As I,

Your creation,

With

Repentance,

Redemption,

And awakening

CHOOSE TO FORGIVE FROM DAWN.

So Be It

COMMENDATIONS FOR DAWN

My God, my Creator,

I, the traveler of life,

Am journeying

Through obstacles,

Through financial difficulties,

Through physical pain,

And through the criticisms

Of this world's unjust voices,

Yet I only worship You.

I only lean on You.

I only fear You.

I only follow Your given commandments.

I love all Your humans,

As You have asked, sought,

And knocked on us to do,

With kindness and understanding.

I know at all corners of life,

And even in death,

My God, You are there.

When I fall,

You are there to hold me,

And to place me back on my feet.

When I cry,

You are there catching my tears.

When I hurt,

You are there erasing my pain.

Through my faith,

I find You.

Through my hope,

I hold on to You.

Through my love for You,

And Your love for me,

We are connected eternally.

As I ask, seek, and knock

On my own faith,

My own hope,

And my own inner door of love,

I find all the answers.

Through all the obstacles of life,

I shall never go astray.

I shall never hurt anyone

Through criticism,

Or through inflicting

Any physical or emotional pain.

I know the pain of the sufferers

As I have been there.

SPIRITUAL SONGS V: DAWN THROUGH DUSK

So, as I see the first sight of light,

I pray never to be

The person or cause

That has caused pain.

I shall be the silent voice

Of the understanding,

Not the voice that causes pain.

My God, give me the strength.

My God, provide me the grace,

The love, and the mercy

All Your humans seek and need.

May I be the bridge

Of common ground,

Common understanding,

And fairness.

May my prayers reach all the critics

And the supporters

As I take the vows

To be truthful,

To be just,

To honor all,

And to love all as my

COMMENDATIONS FOR DAWN.

So Be It

CONTENTMENT FROM DAWN

Diligently I work

With all earnings

As my gifts from grace.

I pray to never forget my blessings,

Never lose my footings of where I come from,

And never overburden myself

But live within my means.

Oh my God,

I pray to You for guidance,

For protection,

And for honor to bless me

With the means of this world

To provide a plate full of food

For my family,

A shelter over their heads,

And clothing for them.

I never lose faith

As I believe my God provides for all

As we ask, seek, and knock to be content

And have

CONTENTMENT FROM DAWN.

So Be It

COURAGE FROM DAWN

The weak and frail fall

From being put down,

Let down, and let go

From the powerful treatments of the wrong.

Oh my God,

I ask,

I seek,

And I pray

For those who have no one,

For those who have nothing,

And for those who feel lost

Within this world

Where only the rough,

The vigorous, and the unjust rule.

Oh my God,

I ask You to be with the wronged,

Against the wrong,

And be their voice,

Be their power,

And be their

COURAGE FROM DAWN.

So Be It

DARKNESS VANISHES AT DAWN

My God, my Creator,

Hold my hands.

My God, my Creator,

Give me strength.

My God, my Creator,

Show me the way.

My God, my Creator,

Create a path for me.

My God, my Creator,

Even when there is no path, I hold on to You.

My God, my Creator,

I hold on to my faith.

My God, my Creator,

I know and I believe

You will build a bridge for me.

My God, my Creator,

You will take me across over all troubles.

My God, my Creator,

With this prayer,

I know

DARKNESS VANISHES AT DAWN.

So Be It

DAWN APPEALS

Oh my God,

The Omnipotent,

Dawn smiles

As darkness

Fades away

On this beautiful day.

May I,

Your devotee,

Pray,

Worship,

Praise,

And

Love

Only You.

So, I say

Blessed be the day,

And blessed be the prayers

Of each

And every minute

I spend with

Only You

As I pray.

Oh my God,

The Omnipotent,

As darkness falls

And the Sun

Fades away,

May I,

Your devotee,

Not fall prey

To any lost path,

To any obstacles,

Or to any sins.

Oh my God,

The Omnipotent,

Through my prayers,

May I,

Your devotee,

Be guided

Out of the darkness

To the first glimpse of light.

May I never

Forget to pray,

So, I recite my

DAWN APPEALS.

So Be It

DAWN BREAKS OPEN

As the dark times approach,

I see how divided

We the humans are.

Oh my God, my Creator,

We are divided

Through religion,

Through race,

Through color,

And through creed.

Yet I know

My God created

All humans,

All colors,

And all races

To unite us

Into one

Human family.

My God wanted

All His different creations

To love one another,

As we see how unique and special,

Differences amongst us

Make us.

Yet my God,

We the humans have created

Different religions.

We have created

Divisions.

We have created

Superiorities and inferiorities.

We have created a rift

And made

The bridge of union,

The bridge of humanity,

The bridge of

Love,

Faith,

Hope,

Honor,

And grace

Collapse

Through hate and division.

Yet my God, my Creator,

The Omnipotent,

The Omnipresent,

The Omniscient,

You had created

One race, Your human race.

I pray to You,

My God, my Creator,

To take all of

Your humans back onto

The bridge of

Love,

Faith,

Hope,

Honor,

And grace.

Wherever and whichever

House of worship

We enter,

May the pure prayers,

Of all the worshippers

From all different houses

Of worship

Reach only You.

As we are divided,

We have gone astray.

We have walked

Upon the wrong path,

Yet You were,

And always stand upon

The right path,

The right place,

The right house,

As everything happens

On Your command.

All wrong shall

Be corrected,

And all mistakes,

Shall be forgiven

At Your command.

The lost

And stranded

Walkers

Will find their way

Back to You,

Through Your

Command

As I know

And believe,

Through Your command,

DAWN BREAKS OPEN.

So Be It

DAWN PETITION

Oh my God,

The Omnipotent,

The Omnipresent,

The Omniscient,

As dawn breaks open

In the vast skies,

I wake up

And remember to pray.

I pray with all

My heart,

My mind,

My body,

And my soul.

May all obstacles

Be it physical pain,

Be it emotional pain,

Or be it obstacles

As huge as a mountain,

May all of it disappear

Like the morning fog.

I pray oh my God,

May we find

Blessings,

Mercy,

And forgiveness.

May we

Be safe,

Be healthy,

Be wealthy,

Be happy,

And manifest

Only positive energies.

Let the negative energies

Disappear

Like the morning fog.

May the first light

Of daybreak

Make us

Overcome all obstacles,

As after darkness

Comes daybreak.

So, with complete faith,

I pray at this daybreak,

My

DAWN PETITION.

So Be It

DAWN PRAYER

My Lord, my Creator,

The dark night's struggles end

With the

Shining smile of dawn.

I greet

Your blessed Sun

As he shines

And pours blessings

Upon Your Earth.

He removes darkness

Through his miraculous devotion.

My Lord,

I pray to You

To remove all the obstacles,

All the darkness,

And bless me.

My Lord,

Today,

With Your miraculous touch,

Bless this world

With a glorious dawn.

My Lord,

With Your blessed miracles,

Remove all curses

And all negative prayers

Sent to You

From others.

With this prayer,

I, Your devotee,

Ask,

Seek,

And knock

Upon Your mercy

To bless me

On this Earth today

For I only worship You.

I only call upon You.

Please my Lord,

Bless me

On this day.

May my words,

My prayers,

Be answered

And be found

By all

Around the globe

As a gift of peace

And happiness.

May my words,

My prayers,

Be answered

To find

A bridge connecting

All humans

From this world

To You,

The Omnipotent,

The Omnipresent,

The Omniscient,

My Lord,

My Creator,

My God.

As my prayers are

My only way

Of communication

With You,

My God,

Answer and accept my

DAWN PRAYER.

So Be It

DAWN THROUGH DAWN IS ONE LIFE

My God,

The Giver of my life,

I pray within this life,

May I appreciate

My life.

May I love

My life.

May I always smile

In life.

May I learn to live

My life.

My God created all life,

For He loves

To give life.

He smiles

Through life.

He appreciates all life

For He is the Creator of life

And He reminds

All living life,

DAWN THROUGH DAWN IS ONE LIFE.

So Be It

DAWN, SO BE IT

When I find myself

Lost and stranded,

I know all shall be

Just all right,

As I know,

My Lord is there.

So, I say,

So be it.

When my physical pain

Throbs,

And I feel

I cannot take it anymore,

I know all shall be

Just all right,

As I know,

My Lord is there.

So, I say,

So be it.

When I find

My financial burdens

Overwhelm me,

I know all shall be

Just all right,

As I know,

My Lord is there.

So, I say,

So be it.

When I find myself

Crying for protection

From the prowling

Predators of this world,

I know all shall be

Just all right,

As I know,

My Lord is there.

So, I say,

So be it.

When I need to find

My purpose in life,

To be heard,

And as I find myself

Crying,

I know all shall be

Just all right,

As I know,

My Lord is there.

So, I say,

So be it.

When and where

Everything is lost,

And nothing is found,

Where I need guidance,

I need support,

And I need direction

Through

The journey of life,

I know all shall be

Just all right,

As I know,

My Lord is there.

So,

With complete

Faith

And

Devotion,

I say,

From dawn through

Dusk through

DAWN, SO BE IT.

So Be It

DAWN'S BLESSINGS

Scattered paints

Lay upon the palette

Of my God,

My Creator.

He gently colors

The skies,

The Earth,

The celestial beings,

The universe,

And all the creations

Above and beyond.

Throughout time and tide,

Everything changes

As humans live upon Earth

And go beyond,

Yet the Painter's palette

Remains the same.

The skies,

The oceans,

The green grass,

The snow-covered mountain tops,

And the sand-covered deserts

Never change.

We the humans today,

The humans of the past,

And the humans in the future

Have, had, and shall

Witness the same

Miracle upon Earth.

The biggest miracle

Of my God,

My Creator,

The Painter

Of everything that exists,

Is nothing but a miracle

As we see

In front of us

The dark night disappears,

And reappears the daylight

Painted from the color palette

Of the one and only God,

The Omnipotent,

As His blessings

Upon us the creation,

DAWN'S BLESSINGS.

So Be It

EMBRACE FORGIVENESS FROM DAWN

Oh my God,

I invite You

With my mind,

My body,

And my soul,

So I can,

Oh my God,

Ask You

To hold me

And take me

Through the path

Which has been

Bestowed

With

Your forgiveness.

Oh my God,

Remove me

From the path

Which You have

Forsaken

And no

Forgiveness

Finds its way.

Oh my God,

Through this prayer

I knock upon

Your door

Of mercy.

Through my faith,

My hope,

And my belief,

Take me

Onto the path,

You have decorated

With forgiveness,

As I eternally

Will ask forgiveness

To be bestowed

Upon me

And all

Your creation

Who pray

And

EMBRACE FORGIVENESS FROM

DAWN.

So Be It

FIRST GLIMPSE OF DAWN

I pray to

My God,

The Omnipotent,

The Merciful,

The Forgiver,

The Giver of sustenance,

The Healer.

Please,

Accept my prayer.

I pray only to You.

I worship only You

From the first

Break of dawn,

Through

The first sign of sunset,

And through

The dark night's

Unknown

Prowling fears.

I never stop praying,

As I call upon

You,

My God,

My Creator,

The Omnipotent.

I fear not

The forbidden sins,

As I have my faith,

My belief,

And my hope

Carrying me

Throughout time

With Your blessings

Within Your protection.

All my fears

And all my worries

Through my hope,

My belief,

And my faith,

Become ashes.

Throughout

Everything,

This fearless soul

Of mine,

For my love for You,

Stands with

My hands in salutation,

My head bowed down,

And my mind,

Body,

And soul

With devotion

In prayer

To You.

I have

Within my mind,

Body,

And soul,

The blessings

And

Glad tidings

Of my God,

The Omnipotent.

Through my belief,

I find I am

Not in the darkness,

But in front of

The

FIRST GLIMPSE OF DAWN.

So Be It

FIRST SUPPLICATION OF DAWN

My God,

The Omnipotent,

The Creator of all

Above and beyond,

Through the frightening

Thunderstorm-filled skies,

I ask You to help me

Through the obstacles of life.

My God,

This life of mine is Your gift.

This mind, body, and soul,

That I travel upon Earth with,

Are Your creations.

From Your hands,

I was created.

From Your breath,

I breathe.

From Your will,

I am here.

Oh my God,

The Merciful,

The Forgiver,

The Giver,

The Just,

I pray to You

For guidance,

For sustenance,

For good health,

For love,

And for prosperity.

My life is a path

Filled with hurdles,

Where blockages are found

At all corners.

On this hard,

Obstacle-filled path,

How do I find a solution?

Where do I find a helping hand?

I pray,

My God,

Take my hands.

Walk me to the place I must be at.

Guide me to the people I must be with.

Oh my God,

I ask,

I seek,

And I knock

On Your door for help

For I am Your devoted

And beloved creation

Who has lost my footings.

I have lost my way and my path.

All around me, fog has appeared,

Clouding my path.

Thunder covers up my calls for help.

Drenching rain freezes my feet

To the ground.

Oh my God,

Take me upon

Your blessed mercy,

And remove all my hurdles.

As the glowing light shines

Through my windows

And kisses my head,

May my prayers too,

Through the same windows,

Reach You,

As my

FIRST SUPPLICATION OF DAWN.

So Be It

FOR ME AT DAWN

My God,

My Creator,

The Omnipotent,

I raise my hands together.

I lift my head up

Toward the skies,

And I seek,

I knock,

And I ask for only You.

Please hear

My prayers.

Oh my God,

The Omnipresent,

I raise my hands

Together,

I bow my head down

Toward the blue ocean

As I call,

I search,

And I wait for only You.

Oh my God,

The Omniscient,

I keep myself

Closed,

My eyes

Closed,

And my mouth

Closed

As I walk through the pain,

The suffering,

And the hurdles of life.

With hope,

With faith,

And with a wish

In my mind,

My body,

And my soul,

When there is no one,

When there is no way,

When there is no hope,

Oh my God,

My Creator,

Please do not ever leave me.

Be there

FOR ME AT DAWN.

So Be It

FOREVER PROTECTED FROM DAWN

As the Sun rises
And I get out of bed,
I begin my day as I pray
With complete faith, complete hope,
Complete grace, and with complete love,
May my loved ones and I be safe,
Be healthy, be wealthy, and be wise.
I pray may I always be loyal,
Always be faithful,
Always be honest,
And always be humble.
I pray may I never go astray,
Never touch the deadly sins,
Never be disloyal,
And never give up on my commitments.
Oh my God,
As the day will come to an end,
I pray may I be within Your blessing,
Within Your mercy, Your forgiveness,
And within Your hands,
FOREVER PROTECTED FROM DAWN.

So Be It

FORGIVENESS AT DAWN

The days are short

And the nights are shorter.

Time flies by

And the waves wash away.

Oh my God,

I see Your creation

Who were standing upon Earth,

Who were walking, talking, and laughing,

Are now one by one

In the departure lounge.

I, Your creation, wait with

Baggage filled with burdens,

Heart filled with regrets,

Mind filled with remorse,

Body filled with penitence,

And soul filled with repentance.

I ask, seek,

And knock on Your mercy

To accept my redemption,

And bestow upon me

FORGIVENESS AT DAWN.

So Be It

FORGIVING GRACEFUL GLOW OF DAWN

Oh my God,

Today,

I am a sinner

Lost in the world

Where

I ask,

I seek,

And

I knock,

On Your

Door of mercy,

Your door of forgiveness,

And Your door of grace.

Forgiveness I seek

Through

Repentance,

Redemption,

And awakening.

I know

For me

There is no way of

Knowing,

Seeing,

Or hearing

If I am the forgiven,

For I know

Where there is no one,

Where there is nothing,

And there is no direction,

I have You.

I am the lost,

Yet I am not afraid

As my God is my direction.

My God is my path.

My God is my Creator.

I believe and know

Through all my prayers,

My God

Is the Forgiver

Who forgives

As He removes

All my darkness

And all my sins

Through His

FORGIVING GRACEFUL GLOW OF DAWN.

So Be It

ANN MARIE RUBY

FORGOT TO PRAY AT DAWN

Oh my God,

The Omnipotent,

The Creator of all creations,

The Creator of the solar system,

And all that is above and beyond,

Forgive me.

You keep

Everything in routine,

Everything on time in a system,

Yet I, Your creation,

Am tired,

Am rushing,

And am trying to cope

With the burdens of life.

I try to finish all the chores

I must finish.

I try to manage my days and my nights

Through worries,

And the obstacles

I must overcome,

I must face,

I must cross through life.

SPIRITUAL SONGS V: DAWN THROUGH DUSK

I try to complete everything in a day,

But this morning,

I forgot the most important job,

The most beautiful thing,

The only part of this life's action

I find comforting,

I find relaxing,

I find spirit lifting,

The only thing that removes

All my worries,

All my obstacles,

All my anger,

And all my sorrows.

Oh my God,

The Omnipotent,

The Omnipresent,

The Omniscient,

Please forgive me as today,

The burdens of this world

Overburdened my soul,

My mind, and my body

So I, Your beloved creation,

FORGOT TO PRAY AT DAWN.

So Be It

FORTITUDE FROM DAWN

My God,

My Creator,

Today,

I pray for valor

To have during

The times of danger.

Oh my God,

I pray for bravery

To have when

I must protect myself,

My family,

And my friends.

Oh my God,

I ask for determination

To know

How to deal with

All the troubles of life.

I ask for Your mercy

To give me

In the times of pain and adversities,

FORTITUDE FROM DAWN.

So Be It

FROM DAWN THROUGH DUSK

Oh my God,

The Omnipotent,

As dawn approaches,

I hear church bells ring.

I hear humans

Gathering dishes for breakfast.

I hear cars honking.

Oh my God,

The Omnipotent,

Where am I?

As dawn becomes dusk,

I hear church bells ring.

I hear humans singing.

I hear humans brawling.

I hear music playing loudly.

Oh my God,

The Omnipotent,

The smell of

Fresh cooked food,

The joy of

People walking,

And the kind words of

Smiling strangers
Make the streets
A better and safer place.
I ask You,
Oh my God,
The Omnipotent,
Where am I?
As I find the answer,
I am blessed
To be
Upon Your created world.
On my journey,
I travel from
The mountains
Through the ocean
To a street where
Love, laughter, and life
Find a purpose
To live in joy
And harmony.
As all walk
Through the streets of life,
I ask my God,
The Omnipotent,

SPIRITUAL SONGS V: DAWN THROUGH DUSK

Where am I?

As I recite a prayer,

I repeat,

But my God,

The Omnipotent,

I am on the

Road of life,

Road of sins,

Road of curses,

Road of prayers,

Road of forgiveness,

Road of mercy,

And road of death.

That is where

I am upon.

I ask my God,

The Omnipotent,

Where am I?

I answer my own question

Through the journey of my life,

Through this blessed prayer

I recite

FROM DAWN THROUGH DUSK.

So Be It

FROM DAWN THROUGH DUSK THROUGH DAWN

My heart beats

Your name.

My eyes open with

Your smiles.

My mind,

My body,

And my soul,

All night and all day

Only worship You,

My God,

The Omnipotent,

The Omnipresent,

The Omniscient.

My relationship with You began

When You created me.

Oh my God

I travel upon Earth

And within my mind,

My body,

And my soul,

I carry Your name.

Oh my God.

For eternity,

My mind,

My body,

And my soul

Belong only to You

And forever

To You.

With this prayer,

With all my faith,

With all my belief,

And with all my love,

I hope

My love for

The Omnipotent

Spreads all over the skies,

The Earth,

The oceans,

And the souls

Of all Your creation.

In union, we say

We are the creation

Of the Omnipotent

FROM DAWN THROUGH DUSK THROUGH DAWN.

So Be It

FURNISHED AT DAWN

Oh my God,

My Creator,

Your creation's hunger

Finds no reasoning

As the body cries.

The pain in the body

Finds no calmness

As it just hurts.

The missing roof

Over our heads

Finds no protection

From the storms.

Oh my God,

I raise my hands high above

Toward the Heavenly skies

For Your intercession.

I pray for all the needy

On this Earth

To have

Their basic survival needs

FURNISHED AT DAWN.

So Be It

FUTURE AT DAWN

One life

We live on Earth.

My God,

Through this journey,

I pray

I do not fall prey

To the wrong decisions.

May I not get on the wrong path.

May I not act upon the wrong terms

But my God,

Guide me to make

The right decision.

Take me to the right path.

May I act upon the right terms

As our birth is guaranteed.

Our last breath is guaranteed,

Yet our life on Earth is guaranteed

Through our own actions.

So, my God,

I pray for my

FUTURE AT DAWN.

So Be It

GIFT OF LOVE AT DAWN

Oh my God,

My Creator,

The Omnipotent,

The Omnipresent,

The Omniscient,

As I walk through

The dark times in my life,

The dark streets through life,

The dark days that I fear,

I remind

My mind,

My body,

And my soul

To remember

My God,

My Creator,

Will protect me.

I am in His embrace

Through my affection,

My respect,

And my care for my God,

The Benevolent.

Through my eternal love,

My everlasting vows

Shall never go astray.

My passionate beliefs,

Oh my God,

My Creator,

Guide me to never fall prey

To the fears of the dark times.

My faith, my hope, and my love

For my God,

Tie me to my God, my Creator.

This eternal bind

Will protect, save, and shield,

My earthly vehicle,

And make my mind, my body,

And my soul immortal

Through my love

For my God, my Creator.

I pray and sing the songs of my God's

Grace, mercy, and forgiveness

At the first glimpse of light

As my

GIFT OF LOVE AT DAWN.

So Be It

GIFTS OF DAWN

My God, my Creator,
Dawn breaks open
Through Your vast skies,
Yet the skies
Are still dark.
The fog-covered skies
Seem frightful at times.
The minds of us humans
Appear to accept
Or decline them
As our hearts
Cry with worries
This world gives us.
I, Your devoted creation,
Wait for the sunny days
To return to my life.
I wait for a financial break.
I wait for a home
Filled with loved ones.
I wait for a garden
With a white picket fence.
I wait for a healthy and sustainable life

SPIRITUAL SONGS V: DAWN THROUGH DUSK

Where no illness

Is found,

Where a husband and wife

Walk hand-in-hand,

Where the children bring home

Blessed grandchildren,

Where my God is worshipped,

And at all times,

Everyone in the household

Remembers all is but

My God's blessings.

Today,

As I ask, seek, and knock

For my innocent wishes

To come true,

As I wait for the fog

In my life to lift

And bring me a

Brighter sunny day,

I appreciate,

I accept,

And I acknowledge

All that I have

Is a blessing

As all is my Lord's will.

I keep sending

My prayers,

My innocent wishes,

To You, my God,

Above the Heavenly skies.

With my complete faith

And complete belief,

I know my God

Will answer my prayers.

After all the darkness,

All the difficulties,

And all the suffering,

The blessed smiling Sun

Appears as proof.

After all the darkness,

Dawn will reappear.

Prayers will be answered.

My God answers the prayers,

The wishes,

Of His devoted creation

As the

GIFTS OF DAWN.

So Be It

GIVE GRACE AT DAWN

Oh my God,

My Creator,

The Omnipotent,

May we have good health.

Oh my God,

May we have sustenance.

Oh my God,

May we have wisdom,

Oh my God,

May we have love.

Oh my God,

May we have Your mercy.

Oh my God,

May we have Your blessings.

Oh my God,

May all obstacles be removed.

Oh my God,

May You accept our prayers

As we pray

And

GIVE GRACE AT DAWN.

So Be It

GLORY OF DAWN

My God,

As the Sun peeks through and welcomes dawn,

I pray to You, my Creator,

To bless this day,

So that I can be safe,

Be healthy,

Be wealthy,

Be wise,

Be happy,

And always make all around me happy.

May my obstacles be gone

And all my worries disappear

Like the dark night that departs.

With Your touch,

With Your mercy,

With Your blessings,

With Your grace,

And with Your command

Appears each day after the dark night,

The

GLORY OF DAWN.

So Be It

GREETINGS OF DAWN

My God,

My Creator,

I welcome this dawn

With my hands

Held up in prayers.

I close my eyes

Not because

I, Your creation,

Want to remember

The dark night's

Fearful events,

But because I

Want to wipe them away

From my memory.

My God,

Grant me

The patience.

My God,

Grant me

The will.

My God,

Grant me

The energy.

My God,

Grant me

The strength

To deal with

All the miseries

Of yesterday

As I welcome and greet

The new day.

My God,

Grant me

The means

To deal with all the work

I must do on this day.

My God,

Grant me

The opportunity

To find the things

I seek, I knock, and ask for

From only You.

Oh my God,

May I, Your creation,

Never go astray

Or fall prey.

May this world's

Glittering fool's gold

Not tempt me,

But may only

Your mercy,

Your grace,

And Your blessings

Touch me and protect me

Throughout eternity.

I am a creation

Who has been praying

For guidance

I seek from only You.

I knock for only You.

I ask for only

Your love and blessings

To be my guide

During the day

And during the dark nights.

My God,

Hold and protect

My loved ones and me

From all fatalities of life,

From all ill callings,

From all financial

And social obstacles.

May we stand upon

Your path,

Where the path is blessed

With Your grace,

Your mercy,

And Your guidance,

Where no ill shall befall,

No hardships will follow,

As there my Lord,

You smile and say,

It is all Your plan.

I live only

As Your blessed creation

On Your blessed Earth

With You my God,

My Creator,

Eternally in my mind,

My body,

And my soul.

Where You are always present,

My God,

Nothing will go wrong

As my God's will

Is what I shall follow.

All that go wrong

Were my wrong choices.

And all that go right,

Are but my God's blessings.

As I have crossed

The dark night's path,

Holding and leaning on

My God,

The Omnipotent,

I am blessed to say

I have found myself

In a new day.

I greet the

Glorious shining

Morning star

Smiling at me

With a message

From my God,

The Omnipotent,

As

GREETINGS OF DAWN.

So Be It

HOPE FROM DAWN TO DUSK

From sunrise to

Sunset,

I pray to

You,

My God,

The Omnipotent,

To be safe,

To be healthy,

To be wealthy,

And to be wise.

From dawn to

Dusk,

I pray to

You,

My God,

The Omnipotent,

May I

Never go astray,

Never fall prey,

And never lose

HOPE FROM DAWN TO DUSK.

So Be It

HOPEFUL DAWN

I pray to my Creator,

The Omnipotent,

The Merciful,

On this day,

The last day of the year,

For forgiveness,

For mercy,

And for blessings.

May all

The miseries,

May all the obstacles,

May all the mistakes

Committed by me,

Be forgiven.

Oh my God,

May I never go off

Your path,

Your commandments,

Or Your light.

Oh my God,

As I wait

For the new year

ANN MARIE RUBY

To arrive
May I be blessed
With good health, good wealth,
And good luck.
I pray to You
During the dark night
As I join all Your creation
And watch the skies
Which have lit up
With lights, colors,
And sparkles.
All of Your creation celebrate
And I, Your blessed devotee,
Join everyone
With hope,
Faith, and belief.
May all hurdles burn away
As we light up the world
With love, joy, and laughter,
And welcome
A happy new year
With another
HOPEFUL DAWN.

So Be It

HOUSEWARMING GIFTS AT DAWN

My God,

The Provider of sustenance,

The Remover of obstacles,

The one and only Creator

I worship and pray to,

The only One

From whose breath

I breathe,

The Giver of life,

The Taker of life,

I call upon You.

My God, my Creator,

I, Your beloved creation on Earth

Pray to You.

All creation need a shelter

To feel safe within.

I am blessed for

You, my God,

Have bestowed a

Place on Earth for me.

Today, I pray

For Your intervention.

May I find a dwelling
Safe and big enough
For my entire blessed family,
To live and love,
And to cherish and worship only You.
I am grateful
You have blessed me with
A place now,
Yet I ask You, my God, my Creator,
To open the doors
Of my blessed home
I have been waiting for,
Where may my family and I
Thrive and follow
Your laws,
Your commandments,
Your will,
And Your ways.
May we
Not go astray
Or fall prey
To any evil
Within this blessed
And sacred home.

My God, my Creator,

May You

Bestow upon my faith

A blessed home,

Safe and secure from all evil.

I pray from dawn to dusk to dawn

Only to You,

My God, my Creator,

To create one such

Miraculous dwelling

For my family and me,

Where we will reside,

And bless all future generations to reside

And celebrate the glory

Of the Omnipotent,

My God, my Creator.

All my future generations

Upon Earth shall

Only worship You,

Where no sins shall reside,

Where no sinners shall be

As I shall wash the house

And bless the house

With the blessed prayers,

I write only for You.

Oh my God,

I pray

For You to guide us

To this such home.

My God, open our eyes

So, we may have

The knowledge

Of the right house.

Oh my God,

On this path,

And on the path

I shall travel

From now to the day

I find the blessed house,

And as we reside

In the blessed house,

May I have

Your protection,

Your support,

And Your presence

Through the miraculous doors

Which I knock, I ask, and I seek

For my prayers

To reach You.

May my prayers be accepted

As I call You,

My God, my Creator.

Always,

Through my prayers,

I never lose hope or my faith in

My God, my Creator,

The Omnipotent.

For Your love

For Your creation,

And Your creation's love for You,

My God, my Creator,

Create a bridge

Through blessed

And sacred prayers.

Bless me

And all who call

The God, The Omnipotent

For a home,

With Your answers,

As

HOUSEWARMING GIFTS AT DAWN.

So Be It

JOURNEY OF LIFE FROM DAWN

I pray to

My God,

The Omnipotent,

Protect us,

Your beloved creation,

Who call only You

And who worship only You

From all obstacles.

My God,

The Omnipotent,

Guide us,

Your beloved creation,

To safety

So we make the right choices

Where we must choose

And when we do not see

The path ahead of us,

My God,

My Creator,

Throughout this

JOURNEY OF LIFE FROM DAWN.

So Be It

LANTERN OF DAWN

Oh my God,

The Omnipotent,

Protect me,

Save me,

Guide me,

And heal me eternally.

My God, my Creator,

Keep me

Within Your embrace,

Within Your grace,

Within Your mercy,

And within Your blessings.

Even though I,

My God,

Am on Earth,

You,

My God, my Creator,

Are forever on Earth beneath,

And Heavens above,

As You are the Omnipresent,

The Merciful,

And the Forgiver.

My only path to You is through

My repentance, redemption, and awakening.

With this prayer,

I the repentant creation,

Ask, seek, and knock on Your mercy.

Please my God, save me,

And protect me

From all the hindrances,

All the hurdles,

And all the troubles of life.

I pray with all my hope,

And with all my faith

To be blessed

Through Your grace.

Oh my God,

I pray may I,

With Your guidance,

Be touched with

Your brightest

Forgiveness, acceptance, and mercy,

As You send upon the Earth,

Your

LANTERN OF DAWN.

So Be It

LET DAWN BE VICTORIOUS

Dark cloudy skies

Greet all at dawn.

Oh my God,

The Omnipotent,

I watch the Sun

Shining from

Behind the clouds

Messaging to me

To never give up on hope

As even the Sun

Never gives up.

He shines, smiles,

And says,

Never give up

For I am here.

Even if you do not

See me as the clouds

Cover me,

I see you.

Oh my God,

I, Your creation,

Learn from the Sun

As I know the cliff,

The darkness,

In my life

Too will fade

As I have within my soul,

My hope,

My faith,

And my prayers.

Through the good times

And through the bad times,

I never give up

On hope

As I have with me

My eternal faith that

My God,

My Creator,

You are there

Even if I cannot see You.

My God,

My Creator,

You too

Live above the

High skies

And I upon

Earth below

Holding on to

My faith,

My belief,

And my prayers.

You see me

Even though

I do not see You,

Oh my God,

My Creator,

Yet I recite

My prayers

Only for You.

So, I pray

With complete devotion

And I say,

Oh my God,

My Creator,

Remove

From my life

All darkness

And

LET DAWN BE VICTORIOUS.

So Be It

MARVELOUS DAWN

I pray to my God,

The Omnipotent,

For guidance,

For protection,

And for safety.

I pray to my God,

The Omnipotent,

For sustenance,

For good health,

For stable income,

And for safe housing.

I pray to my God,

The Omnipotent,

To protect the children,

To protect the furry children,

And to protect my twin flame and me.

I pray to my God,

The Omnipotent,

To keep me

On the right path,

To protect me

Against all evil

And to protect me

From all hurdles.

I pray to my God,

The Omnipotent,

May I never

Go astray,

May I never

Fall prey to any sins,

And may I always

Be within Your embrace.

I pray to my God,

The Omnipotent,

To keep me within

Your grace,

To keep me within

Your mercy,

And to keep me within

Your blessings

Through sunrise and sunset,

Through the dark night's travels,

And through the arrival of

The

MARVELOUS DAWN.

So Be It

MAY VICTORY BE TO DAWN

As the new year

Arrives upon

All creation,

I pray to my God,

The Omnipotent,

The Omnipresent,

The Omniscient.

May the first light of the new year

Burn away all darkness

From the lives of Your creation

Who reside

Upon this world.

Oh my God,

I pray

Through this

Prayer

For all Your creation

Across the world

Who through a prayer,

Pray for all evil

To be removed,

Who pray for all obstacles

To be removed,

And who pray for financial difficulties

To be removed.

I pray for all who pray

For physical illnesses

To be removed.

I pray for all who pray

For all human ignorance

To be removed

Through faith, hope,

And belief.

May a prayer recited from the minds,

The bodies, and the souls,

Of all creation

Across all nations

Be accepted.

As we light our candles

And recite blessed prayers

To diminish all darkness

From all minds, bodies, and souls

Across the world,

We pray

MAY VICTORY BE TO DAWN.

So Be It

MEDITATION OF DAWN

My God,

You are the Creator of the minds

Through which we define

Our consciousness.

You, my God, are

The Creator of the physical bodies

Through which we are

Living and breathing.

You, my God, have created

The physics,

The matter,

The properties,

And the non-living things.

With all things combined,

I, Your creation, meditate

To breathe out all

The negative thoughts

And breathe in only

Positive thoughts.

My God, my Creator,

Help me to discard

All the stress through

Calming myself by

Meditating to You,

My God, my Creator.

I know my mind,

My body,

And my soul

Only worship You.

I know

By reciting Your name,

Through faith, hope, and complete belief,

I can detoxify

And let go of all the stress

My body and my mind pick up

As my soul is always

Stress-free

And with only You.

So today,

I let go of all my stress,

As I know You have said

Not to walk ahead

In my life with stress,

For only You know

What is ahead, not I.

Why worry about things

That are not,

And worry about things

That cannot be changed?

I shall only

Believe in the good

And the powers

Of my God, my Creator,

By not giving

Power to my thoughts,

But giving power back

To God,

The Remover of all obstacles.

God the Creator

Loves His creation

And shall walk

With us through

All obstacles of life.

He shall be with us,

Through the path of grief,

And through the path of joy and mercy.

He will be there with us

Eternally.

So, we should carry

Within

Our minds,

Our bodies,

And our souls,

Faith and belief,

And know

To let go of the stress

We create and pick up

Through the

Obstacles of life.

May I learn to be happy in life,

Not overwhelmed by it.

Let me worry through the

Obstacles but not be

Overburdened by them.

I shall lay my faith on

The knowledge of my God,

My Creator's existence.

Throughout my time on Earth

Or beyond,

I shall do my best

To have on my plate of life,

Good deeds.

I shall try to erase

The bad deeds for I am

Your creation,

Who knows not the future,

Who knows not what shall happen,

And who knows not what shall not happen.

Yet I know my God,

My Creator,

The All-Knowledgeable,

Knows my past, my present,

And my future.

My God knows

My mind's thoughts,

My body's actions,

And the physics

Of all that is around me.

So, I shall with this knowledge

Let go of all my worries.

My stress shall no more

Burden my mind,

My body,

Or my soul.

Just like the dark night

That evaporated,

The darkness from

All around me

Is also erased

As the Sun too shines

Upon my skies.

Taking

The powerful name

Of my God,

My Creator,

I awoke at the

First kiss of dawn.

I find myself stress-free,

Relaxed,

And rejuvenated.

I breathe in all that is good,

And breathe out

All the stress of this life.

Today,

At the first sight of dawn,

I witness the

Amber glow of the

Golden Sun,

Interceding for me,

Through the

MEDITATION OF DAWN.

So Be It

MIRACULOUS AT DAWN

My God the Merciful,

My God the Forgiver,

My God the Giver,

This dawn,

I, Your creation,

Am lost and stranded,

Confused and lonely,

Waiting for a miracle

To break through.

Oh my God,

May there be mercy for me

On this Earth.

May I be forgiven for

The known and unknown sins

I have committed

On this Earth.

May I be blessed

With Your hands,

And be given

Some love

And some kindness

On this Earth.

I know all the humans

Upon Earth

See themselves and their own.

I have no one

To ask,

To seek,

Or to knock upon

For my miraculous gifts.

So,

I ask,

I seek,

And I knock upon You,

The Omnipotent,

The Omnipresent,

The Omniscient,

To open the door of

Mercy, forgiveness, and giving.

Through Your blessings,

May I too get the miracle I wait for

As I call upon You,

My God,

The

MIRACULOUS AT DAWN.

So Be It

MIRACULOUS SUSTENANCE OF DAWN

My God, my Creator,

I walk

Through the difficulties,

Through the obstacles,

And through no solutions found,

On this gray and windy day.

As I raise my hands in prayers

To only You,

I ask

My God, my Creator,

Please remove

This heavy burden

From my life.

I am walking

Through the path of life,

Where all say

To accept destiny

And give up on hope,

Give up on faith,

And give up on all my beliefs

As they only pour

Tears of heartache.

They shower and drench
My mind, my body, and my soul
With only disappointments.
As I struggle
Through all my hardships,
All my physical and emotional pain,
I light my candles of hope.
I walk into a church,
I walk into a synagogue,
I walk into a mosque,
I walk into a temple,
And I realize
All of Your creation
From all different houses of faith
Gather in their own houses of worship,
And raise their hands
To You in prayer.
In different ways,
Through different words
And languages,
Yet they are all
Faithfully praying
To You,
Oh my God, my Creator.

I see the pain, the tears, and the sufferings

All of their inner hearts

Are going through.

Their prayers

Said in different languages,

And different

Houses of worship

Touch my inner soul.

Oh my God,

How is it that

Listening and holding on to

All different faiths could be so wrong,

If it feels so right

For they are all Your creation?

My God, my Creator,

My tears fall

As they cannot be caged.

They are free birds

Who fly without restrictions.

Oh my God, my Creator,

I stand under

The biggest roof,

The Heavenly skies.

I stand within not any home

That is closed up,

But upon Your grounds

Open to all on Your Earth,

Created by not humans,

But You,

My God, my Creator.

I ask,

I seek,

And I knock

Upon Your doors

And upon Your mercy,

As I give You a direct call

Through my prayers.

I recite,

Oh my God, my Creator,

The Creator

Of all humans,

Remove all my financial burdens.

Remove all my physical burdens.

Remove all my fears.

Remove all my worries.

Let me

And all who recite this prayer

Be blessed

By You
As I, Your devoted creation,
Write and recite
This prayer for myself
And all others
Who have nowhere to go,
Who have no one
To guide them,
Who have no helping hands
On this Earth,
But You,
My God, my Creator.
Today,
I walk out of
This dim and dangerous road
Through my faith,
Not in any humans,
But only You.
Praying not within any walls,
But upon Your Earth
To help me,
Guide me,
And take me to the place
That is blessed

By You,

The home

That was chosen by You,

The work that has been created

For me by only You.

Oh my God, my Creator,

I stand upon

The biggest and open prayer house,

Your Earth.

I stand under the only roof

You have created

That is now shining

With the bright Sun peeking through

In front of me.

I stand on the path

You have made for me

That tells me to walk forward.

Waiting for me

To fulfill all my wishes

Through my faith

And my glowing hope,

Is the

MIRACULOUS SUSTENANCE OF DAWN.

So Be It

MORNING GLORIES OF DAWN

Oh my Lord,

Bless us on this day

With love,

Affection,

Mercy,

And kindness.

Bless us

With sustenance,

Good health,

And prosperity.

I, Your creation,

Remind myself,

The examples of

The journey of life

My Lord has gifted us

Through the miraculous

Glorious nature.

I know my Lord,

Life is transient

As everything

That starts too must end.

Sorrows shall end.

Troubles will pass

As the hopeless souls

Will see hope

Renewed in the new dawn.

Nothing is lost

As everything is found

Where and when

My Lord is there.

I know my Lord,

We the creation

Are resilient.

We are hopeful.

We are able

To defy the odds,

And we can challenge

The wrong and be victorious

As we have hope guiding us

Through Your blessings.

I know my Lord,

There is nothing

That is hopeless,

As You have shown the truth.

Your symbolic flowers defy even death

As they return to life

In the new dawn.

With hope and with faith

As our companions,

We the creation are taught

To watch and follow the life journey

Of the divine flowers.

They teach us

To never lose hope

Even when everything

Seems hopeless.

This message is sent each dawn

From Your divine flowers

Which tilt and wilt

During the dark night's struggles.

Yet as the Sun reappears,

So do these miraculous flowers.

Defying death,

They are reborn.

My Lord,

We the creation

Know and learn from them

As we call them,

MORNING GLORIES OF DAWN.

So Be It

NEVER FEAR AS DAWN IS HERE

Oh my God,

My Creator,

The Omnipotent,

Please hold on to me.

Give me strength.

Give me faith.

Give me resilience

To walk through life,

Never losing my faith

As life is filled with difficulties.

With every few steps,

I encounter hardships,

Yet I keep walking.

Then again,

My walk is blocked off

With a barrier.

Oh my God,

With faith,

I find ways to keep going.

Oh my God,

I devised and strategized,

To remove all impediments

Through praying

And believing

In myself,

My prayers,

And my path.

I have on this path,

The glad tidings

Of my God,

My Creator,

Who will remove all

My stumbling blocks.

As I walk

Through the darkness

And into the light

With hope,

With faith,

And with a prayer

Always on my lips,

I recite

And I say,

With every breath,

To

NEVER FEAR AS DAWN IS HERE.

So Be It

NEW DAWN BE

With my hands held up in prayers,

Head bowed down in devotion as the Sun rises,

I pray to my God, my Creator,

The Omnipotent,

The Omnipresent,

The Omniscient,

To help those

Who have no one,

Who are helpless,

Who are belittled,

Who have no money,

Yet who know they have You.

Oh my God,

I pray You

Remove my obstacles,

Remove my burdens,

And remove the blockages

Of my life.

Oh my God,

Guide me

And take me to

Where I belong,

Where I have financial support,

Where I have a place to live,

And where the bridge

To all my solutions is found.

I believe,

I believe,

I believe where

Your blessings,

Your grace,

And Your mercy are,

There I too will find

All the blessed answers

As there,

My destiny will be fulfilled.

I am the precant.

My prayers

Are my saving grace.

They knock

Upon Your door of mercy

For all the obstacles

Of my life to fade,

And let my life's

NEW DAWN BE.

So Be It

NIGHT INTO DAWN

Even when no one sees,

When no one believes,

When no one knows,

I know, I believe, and I see

The miracles and the blessings.

I know, I believe, and I see

The truth that this world,

This universe,

And all the celestial beings

Are only a miracle

Created by the one and only

Creator of all creations,

My God, my Creator,

The Omnipotent.

Oh my God,

I believe life,

Death,

All that is,

And all that is not

Is all Your blessing.

You can give

And You can take life.

All is nothing
But Your blessing
For as You say,
Blessed be,
So be it,
Or may it be so,
Everything
And
Anything
Is possible.
As You show all how You,
My God,
My Creator
Can take all into darkness
And bring all back into light,
I know and believe
Through Your blessings,
Anything is possible,
As this morning,
I see
You convert with Your will,
NIGHT INTO DAWN.

So Be It

OLIVE BRANCHES FROM DAWN
THROUGH DUSK THROUGH DAWN

My God, my Creator,

The Omnipotent,

The Creator of the universe,

Bless me, Your creation,

With good health, wealth, and prosperity.

May this day

Wipe away all my sins.

May the known and unknown sins not punish me,

But let this repentant,

This redemptive soul be forgiven.

May all my children,

My future generation,

Be forgiven and be blessed

Through my devotional gift.

May my love for my Lord

And my Lord's love for me

Protect, honor, and save all my dynasty

From today till the end.

Oh my Lord,

Let my blessed home open

Its door to my dynasty.

Let sustenance be given,

163

So my twin flame and I,

Our children,

Our grandchildren,

And their twin flames,

All can grow within

This blessed home.

Bless my prayers

As my prayers are my strength

And my belief.

My Lord

Hears,

Listens,

Sees,

And answers all prayers

Coming from the inner soul.

Oh my Lord,

I pray all future generations

Born from my tree of life,

Today and eternally

Shall always be protected

Within my

OLIVE BRANCHES FROM DAWN THROUGH DUSK

THROUGH DAWN.

So Be It

OMNIPOTENT FROM DAWN THROUGH DUSK THROUGH DAWN

Oh my God,

The Omnipotent,

The Omnipresent,

The Omniscient,

From the first breath

To the last,

May I only worship You.

Oh my God,

From the first light of the day

Through the first glimpse of darkness,

May I only

Worship You.

Oh my God,

I give my salutation

Only to You,

As I see You

In the skies.

I see You

On Earth.

I see You

Within the ocean.

I see You

In my mind,

My body,

And my soul.

Oh my God,

The sacred

And pure love

Of mine

For You

Spread from

My mind,

My body,

And my soul

To all of Your creation

Eternally.

I only pray to You

Forever with

All my breath,

And even when

I have no breath,

I shall pray and worship only

The

OMNIPOTENT FROM DAWN THROUGH DUSK

THROUGH DAWN.

So Be It

PEACE AND HARMONY FROM DAWN

Unsettled waves

Of humanly storms

Touch the creation

Upon Earth.

People walk

In all different directions,

Declaring their victories.

Yet oh my God,

My Creator,

There are differences.

There are so many paths.

All say they are right

And the others

Are wrong.

Then I ask You,

My Creator,

The Omnipotent,

Why this fight?

Why this disagreement?

Why so much unsettlement?

There is only

One world.

There is only

One way

Into this world

And one way

Out of this world.

So, I pray may

We, the creation,

For the harmony

And blessings

Of one another,

For the love

And respect

Of one another,

I pray may we,

The creation

For the

One God,

Our Creator,

The Omnipotent,

Promise to live

With one another

In

PEACE AND HARMONY FROM DAWN.

So Be It

POURING RAINDROPS AT DAWN

Oh my God,

My Creator,

Your dawn broke open

As Your skies

Poured down

Heavenly waters

Upon Your Earth.

The paths became slippery.

The travelers got drenched,

And were freezing cold,

Yet I accept

All of this

As Your grace

And Your blessings

For Your creation.

The Earth smiles

As she was thirsty.

The trees smile

As they were thirsty

And dry.

Your rivers smile

As they were drying out.

The humans complain

As they think

This is an obstacle.

My God,

My Creator,

I, Your devoted creation,

With my mind, body, and soul

In complete devotion,

Know and understand,

Obstacles are just that,

Obstacles,

Which will

Evaporate and disappear

As I patiently pray

To the Creator

Of all creation.

With my mind, body, and soul

In complete devotion

In devotional prayer,

I realize

It is You,

My God,

My Creator,

Who places

Obstacles

On our paths,

At times,

As a caution sign

To be careful

For danger lies ahead

On this path.

It is then I say to all

Who say

My God,

My Creator,

Does not hear,

Does not see,

And does not understand

The pain

Of His creation,

He does,

And He loves all so much.

My God,

My Creator,

Through Your pouring rain,

I pray

Through this journey,

Wash away

All the obstacles
And all the hurdles
From my path.
Grace me
With Your grace.
Forgive me with
Your forgiveness.
Bless me with
Your blessed hands.
My God,
My Creator,
As Your skies pour
Heavenly waters,
I know and realize,
Your blessings are
Being poured from
The Heavens above
To the Earth beneath,
Even though
All Your humans
May think
They are just
POURING RAINDROPS AT DAWN.

So Be It

PRAY FROM DUSK TO DAWN TO DUSK

As dawn first peeks through,

I pray to

You,

My God,

The Omnipotent,

For forgiveness,

For guidance,

For protection,

For sustenance,

For good health,

And for everything

In life

And ever after.

I,

Your creation,

Know I must pray.

Where there is no mercy,

You forgive me.

Where there is no path,

You guide me.

Where there is no safety,

You protect me.

Where there is no food,

You give me sustenance.

Where there is illness,

You heal me.

Where there is no hope,

You give me faith.

Where there is fear,

You give me comfort.

Where there is hardship,

You give me resilience.

Where there is nothing,

You,

My God,

Are there.

So today

And tomorrow,

And for eternity,

For my love

For You,

And Your love

For me,

I

PRAY FROM DUSK TO DAWN TO DUSK.

So Be It

PRAYERS OF THE FAITHFUL
AT DAWN

Oh my God,

My Creator,

All creation

Above Earth

From all different houses,

Raise our hands

As we are lost.

We are hopeless as

We are divided

Through confusion.

Oh my God,

The Omnipotent,

I pray to You.

Please accept us

Who ask, seek,

And knock

On Your doors

As our combined

Prayers are

PRAYERS OF THE FAITHFUL AT DAWN.

So Be It

PROTECTED FROM DAWN

Oh my God,

The sky

Is dark.

The clouds

Are turning gray.

The Earth beneath

Is getting poured upon.

The thunder is

Screaming.

The lightning bolts

Are firing up,

And we,

Your creations,

The humans

And

The animals,

Are going

Down on

Our knees

As we

Look

To the skies above

And place our hands together.

Unitedly,

We say,

A prayer.

Oh God,

Our Creator,

The Omnipotent,

The Omnipresent,

The Omniscient,

Protect us.

Save us.

Give us shelter.

Keep us safe

From all the known

And

Unknown storms of life.

Oh God,

From dawn

Through dusk

Through dawn,

Keep us

Always

PROTECTED FROM DAWN.

So Be It

PROTECTION FROM DAWN THROUGH DUSK

Oh my God, my Creator,

My Protector,

You are the only hope

I have within the Heavens above,

On Earth beneath,

And beyond.

Without You,

I have no one,

No place,

No support to go to or hold on to.

Oh my God,

I seek protection in You

From all the seen, unseen,

Known, and unknown dangers

This life places upon my life.

My God, help me.

My God, guide me.

My God, protect me

Through the journey

Of my life.

As I keep walking

Onto paths filled with obstacles,

May I never fall prey

Or go off the path

You have blessed for me.

May through all my days,

And all my nights,

I be protected from

All the dangers,

Known, and unknown,

All the frightful and dangerous

Humans breathing,

All the restless souls

That have passed on,

All Your creation

Who have gone astray,

And all the spirits

That roam around freely

To only frighten

Your blessed creation.

Today, I raise my hands

In prayer to You.

I bow my head

And although frightened,

I do not forget to breathe.

With all my strength, all my courage,

And all my determination,

I, Your creation,

Call upon You

As I know I have

No supernatural abilities

To overcome

These supernatural,

Or human created dangers.

Yet I know,

I, Your mortal human,

Have the most powerful

Blessing on Earth,

Or beyond Earth,

And Heavens above,

As I have my blessed prayers.

I have my direct connection to You.

My pure and blessed prayers

Shall veil me,

And protect me

As I pray through

This blessed prayer for

PROTECTION FROM DAWN THROUGH

DUSK.

So Be It

PROVISION OF DAWN

Oh my God,

Traveler I am,

Walking through life,

Trying to stay healthy,

Stay strong,

And stay alive.

Yet within this life,

A traveler needs food,

Needs shelter,

And needs clothing.

So, I ask, I seek, and I knock

On my God's compassion

To provide for all humans

When the needs are there,

Yet the means are inadequate.

Oh my God,

I ask for all the needy

As Your creation

Traveling through life

Require Your

PROVISION OF DAWN.

So Be It

PURE DEVOTION AT DAWN

As dawn glorifies the Earth
With the glitters
Of golden sunshine,
Hope glitters
Upon my eyes.
Tears of hope
Escape my eyes
As I open them
At the break of dawn
To worship only You,
My God, my Creator.
From the first sight of dawn
To the first glitter of
The amazing sunset,
I worship only You,
My God, my Creator.
May my every breath
Be taken with
Only Your name,
As I belong to only You,
My God, my Creator.
With hands in prayer,

As I welcome

A better and brighter new day,

May my words spread

Your love and Your hope,

As my words

Will eternally

Worship only You,

My God, my Creator.

My prayers,

Will call upon You

From dawn through dusk through dawn,

As this devotee

Will keep knocking,

Asking,

And seeking only You,

My God, my Creator.

I will keep sending You

My devotion-filled prayers,

My only way of

Connecting with

My God, my Creator,

As that is a devotee's

PURE DEVOTION AT DAWN.

So Be It

PURPOSE FROM DAWN THROUGH DUSK

Oh my God,

As dawn shines upon the Earth,

I see the light

And I pray to never be lost

Within the hurdles of life.

May I, Your creation,

Not get confused

Or forget where I must be,

How to get there,

When to go there,

And which path to take

As my life is a blessing

From Heavens above.

You have created me

To be in this world.

Oh my God,

I pray with my mind, my body

And my soul,

May You guide me

Toward my life's

PURPOSE FROM DAWN THROUGH DUSK.

So Be It

REJUVENATION POWERS OF DAWN

Dawn peeks through

The dark night's skies,

As I peek out from hiding

Under my blanket of hope.

I awaken and stand up

Holding on to

The blessings of faith.

For now,

As the Sun's

Overpowering rays

Touch the Earth

And the physical bodies

Of Your creation,

My God,

I know like a miraculous cure,

We will find

Good health

Entering our bodies.

As the Sun

Sends kisses upon Earth,

We, Your creation,

Will find peace,

Joy, and laughter

Within our lives.

Oh my God,

My Creator,

With the powers

Of Your blessed Sun's

Powerful glowing rays,

We, Your creation,

Will find upon ourselves,

Families,

And friends,

Living together

In musical harmony.

The fearful dark night's stories

That we lived through

Is a nightmare

We will know we survived

For it will be

Just memories

To guide us and prevent us,

From falling prey again.

As today I see

The golden color

Of the Sun's glare

Smiling at me,

I know my prayers

Have been answered,

And have been accepted

By You,

My God, my Creator.

You have guided me,

And all who seek, ask, and knock

For the answers

To their prayers,

To find

All the answers within

Your grace,

Your mercy,

And Your blessings.

After the dark night's struggles,

Holding on to

The hands of

Hope and faith,

We the believers

Finally receive

And witness the

REJUVENATION POWERS OF DAWN.

So Be It

REMOVE HUNGER FROM EARTH BY DAWN

Oh my God, my Creator,

Your Earth

Grows vegetables.

Your Earth

Grows fruits.

Your Earth

Grows grains.

Your Earth

Asks Heavens above

To pour water

For all the children,

To provide for all Your creation.

Yet my God,

The Omnipotent,

The Omnipresent,

The Omniscient,

Why is it then

Your creation on Earth

Go hungry?

The children

Go to bed

Crying in hunger.

SPIRITUAL SONGS V: DAWN THROUGH DUSK

The mothers place

A stone on their souls

To not show

The children

Their hunger.

The fathers place

A towel around their pain

Hiding their hunger.

Why my God,

On Your Earth

Are Your creation hungry?

Oh my God,

Walking through

This dark and cold night,

I raise my hands

Above the ocean water

And I say,

Oh Father Heavens

Provide water to

The children on Earth.

I stand upon Your

Cold and dark roads of

Mother Earth,

And I pray,

Dear Mother Earth,

Please provide for your

Children on Earth

As they are hungry.

My God, my Creator,

I ask You with

This blessed prayer.

I light a candle.

I walk with

This blessed candle

And pray with my mind, my body, and my soul,

May no one

On Your blessed Earth

Ever go hungry.

Oh my God,

The Giver of sustenance,

I pray with

My simple

And pure words,

Today,

May You,

The Merciful,

REMOVE HUNGER FROM EARTH BY DAWN.

So Be It

RISE ABOVE THE WATER AT DAWN

The ocean waves rise,

As the Moon

Sets upon the ocean.

The cold frigid water

Cuts through my skin.

As I breathe, I take up

All the

Pain,

All the

Suffering,

And all the

Anxieties.

I learn to breathe in

Only positive vibes,

And breathe out

The negative vibes.

I say to myself

Over and over again,

My Lord is there,

As I repeat,

I believe,

I believe,

I believe

My God,

My Creator,

Will never drown me,

Will never let me drown,

And will never leave me alone

As

I believe,

I believe,

I believe

All the

Troubles,

All the

Hurdles,

And all the

Obstacles

Shall drown.

As

I believe,

I believe,

I believe,

I shall

RISE ABOVE THE WATER AT DAWN.

So Be It

SAFE AND PROTECTED FROM DAWN

Oh my God,

Darkness covers all

As danger looms around.

In this dark and dangerous time,

I pray to You

To keep me within

The safe company of the people

Whom You, my God, have favored,

And whom You, my God, have given

Mercy, forgiveness, and blessings.

Let my mind, my body, and my soul

Not fall prey to

The temptation of the tempters.

May I always be blessed

Within the safekeeping of my prayers

Which I shall recite

To keep myself within

The faith, honor, and blessings

Of my God, my Creator,

And be

SAFE AND PROTECTED FROM DAWN.

So Be It

SANCTIFICATION OF DAWN

My God, my Creator,

As I see a glimmer of light

In Your vast skies,

I sit on my knees,

Bow my head,

And raise my hands

In prayer.

Oh my God, my Creator,

The Creator of Heavens above,

And Earth beneath,

I ask,

Seek,

And knock upon Your door

Through my blessed prayers.

I pray for mercy.

I pray for forgiveness.

I pray for guidance.

I pray for protection.

I pray for endurance.

I pray for love.

I pray for financial sustenance.

I pray for a safe home.

I pray for my faith,

My belief,

In You,

My God, my Creator,

To always be complete.

May I never go astray,

May my life

Be complete

With Your blessings,

Your love,

And Your grace.

I pray every day,

As I know

My prayers are

My only saving grace.

So as darkness fades,

At the first sight of dawn,

I give my thanks

To my God,

My Creator,

Through my prayers

As the

SANCTIFICATION OF DAWN.

So Be It

SMILE AT DAWN

Oh my God,

The Omnipotent,

On this foggy,

Cold and chilly day,

I place my hands together.

I close my eyes

As I begin to pray.

Oh my God,

The Omnipresent,

Through my pure prayers,

Through my blessed faith,

Through my humble hope,

And through my devout soul,

I pray for all the fog,

All the darkness,

And all the uncertainty

To be lifted

From my life.

Oh my God,

The Omniscient,

With hope,

Faith,

And the most innocent

And blessed soul,

I pray to my God,

My Creator,

To guide me

And

Take me to

A safe place.

Take me to

The right path.

Take me to

The purest land,

Where I belong

And where I will find

The answers

My heart seeks.

I believe

After the fog,

The darkness,

And the uncertainty fade

Through a pure and blessed prayer,

The Sun shall

SMILE AT DAWN.

So Be It

STRENGTHEN ME FROM DAWN THROUGH DUSK

Darkness falls all around me.

Thunder and lightning strike.

I know it is time

I find protection

And I find a shelter.

I will not fall prey

As I am not afraid.

I know I must protect myself

As my God, my Creator,

Helps those who help themselves.

My God is my saving grace, my salvation,

My hope, and my blessings.

By taking precaution,

I am not the weak

But I am the strong.

I have my God's blessings

And I have my prayers

Through which

My God shall

STRENGTHEN ME FROM DAWN THROUGH DUSK.

So Be It

SUPPLICATION AT DAWN

Oh my Lord, help.

Oh my Lord, guide.

Oh my Lord, protect.

Oh my Lord, preserve.

Oh my Lord, forgive.

Oh my Lord, support.

Oh my Lord, guard.

Oh my Lord, assist.

Oh my Lord, answer my prayers

And never let me go

As I pray to only You,

From dawn to dusk to dawn

To remove all my obstacles,

My fears,

My troubles,

And my hurdles.

Never let me

Fall prey

Or go astray

To any temptation,

Any sins,

Any forbidden path,

Or forbidden ways.

May I always be Yours

And on Your path,

The path,

You my Lord

Have blessed.

With and amongst the people,

You, my Lord,

Have accepted

And forgiven.

May my mind,

My body,

And my soul

Always belong to You,

The Omnipotent,

The Omnipresent.

With all my living breath,

Each day as dawn breaks open,

I shall recite

This blessed prayer to You,

My God, the Omnipotent,

As my

SUPPLICATION AT DAWN.

So Be It

SUSTAIN OURSELVES FROM DAWN

Traveler I am through life on Earth.

Oh my God,

I pray for a job as

I, Your creation,

Within my hands,

Have responsibilities

For my blessed family

You, my God, have blessed me with.

I must place bread on their plates.

Oh my God,

I must provide them with a bed to rest,

And a shelter to be safe within.

Oh my God,

My Creator,

I pray to You for help as You never

Give more burdens than

The mind, the body, and the soul can bear.

So today, I ask You

To provide me and all like me

With a job to

SUSTAIN OURSELVES FROM DAWN.

So Be It

TEMPLE OF GOD FROM DAWN

A temple created

By my God,

My Creator,

The Omnipotent,

Is the vehicle,

I travel

Through life with.

Oh my God,

The Omnipresent,

Help me.

Guide

My earthly vehicle

To be healthy

And to have

Only

Physical and spiritual

Attributes

Blessed by You.

Oh my God,

The Omniscient,

May I,

With the wrong decisions

And wrong choices,

Not damage

My earthly vehicle.

Heal me,

My God,

From all

Physical illnesses.

Heal me,

My God,

From all

Spiritual illnesses.

Bless my mind,

My body,

And my soul,

Oh my God,

My Creator,

To always

Do right

As I honor my mind,

My body,

And my soul

As the

TEMPLE OF GOD FROM DAWN.

So Be It

ANN MARIE RUBY

THIS DAWN I PRAY

For You to show me the way,

Oh my God,

This dawn I pray.

As I am lost,

As I am confused,

As I am unable to decide,

So, for You to show me the way,

Oh my God,

This dawn I pray.

As I am financially drained,

As I am physically tired,

As I am emotionally exhausted,

So, for You to show me the way,

Oh my God,

This dawn I pray.

As dawn converts to dusk,

And dusk awaits dawn,

I wait for my God's answers.

For You to show me the way,

Oh my God,

THIS DAWN I PRAY.

So Be It

THROUGH DAWN

My God, my Creator,

From dawn through dusk

Through dawn,

May I, Your creation,

Not fall prey,

Not go astray,

Not get off track,

And not wander off like a stray.

Oh my God, my Creator,

May this devotee

Not drift away or lose my ground

And fall into

The forbidden world of sins.

May my mind

My body,

And my soul

Always be true, be pure, and be clean.

May my hands not touch

Forbidden sins.

May my lips not utter

Forbidden words.

May my mind be clean

From all dirty thoughts.

May my body know its boundaries

And not fall prey to the temptations

Of the forbidden world.

Oh my God, my Creator,

The Giver of the commandments,

Guide me,

Hold me,

Take me into Your embrace,

And never let me go

For I pray only to You,

For direction,

For protection,

And for safety.

I, Your creation,

Pray to You

From the first sight of dawn through dusk

Through dawn.

May I not be lost or confused.

May I eternally be on Your blessed path.

May my prayers keep me safe

From dawn through dusk

THROUGH DAWN.

So Be It

THROUGH FAITH FROM DAWN

Life places me

Under the

Thunderstorms of life,

Yet like an umbrella,

My God's

Blessed hands

Protect me.

Life shakes the Earth

Beneath my feet,

Yet like an earthquake proof

Metal rod,

My God's

Blessed hands are there.

Life drowns me

Within obstacles,

Yet like a magical canoe,

My God's blessed hands

Float me away to safety.

Oh my God,

I pray

As You,

My Creator,

Have never left me

And never stopped believing

In me,

That I will

Come to You.

Today,

I, Your creation,

Hold on to

Your blessed hands,

For I know our bond

Is tied within

My faith,

My hope,

And my belief,

My God is there,

Yet it is me,

Who needed to believe

In this complete

Truth.

So, today,

I declare

My God is there

THROUGH FAITH FROM DAWN.

So Be It

TODAY'S PRAYER AT DAWN

My God, the Immortal,

I, Your mortal creation,

Need Your guidance

Every single day.

Which path must I walk upon?

I try to follow Your footsteps

As I search for Your direction.

My hands ask

For what work

I should complete

And what I must avoid.

In confusion,

With united hands in prayer,

I ask You,

My God, my Creator,

For answers.

Where shall I find

The answers

To all the questions?

My eyes search for answers,

So, I pray to be able

To seek answers

Through Your sight,

To direct my sight

To the right place.

As I close my eyes

And I pray to You,

Oh my God,

With all the obstacles of life,

I remind myself,

My God will

Never burden me

With more obstacles.

So, I pray for the burdens

To be lightened.

Oh my God,

As I do not want

To ever fail You

Because I cannot carry

The burdens

Through

The journey of my life,

I pray during

The darkest time

Of my life

To never give up

On my faith

And to never lose hope

Through the journey of my life.

May every day

Be a blessing,

And may every night

Be a gift.

As I learn

From all my mistakes

And know

To never lose hope,

To never lose faith,

And to always know

Through all difficulties

Of life,

First and foremost,

I must pray.

So, as this dark time

Passes through reciting a prayer,

With hope and complete faith,

I welcome the new day

As I recite

TODAY'S PRAYER AT DAWN.

So Be It

TRAVELING THROUGH DUSK THROUGH DAWN

My God,

The Omnipotent,

The Giver of life,

And the Taker of life,

Today,

I pray for

The departed souls

Of all family members.

Oh my God,

Let them be in peace.

Let them be happy.

Let them have You.

Let us the living

Know, believe, and have faith

In only You

As Your creation

Must return to You.

Life is only a day,

Where we live and play.

We walk along the lonely night,

And find Your given path,

Your given family,

And Your given friends.

We find Your given mercy,

Your given forgiveness,

And Your given grace.

We do not see You.

We do not hear You.

Yet we know You are there

In the invisible land

We call Heaven,

Where all the living creation

Must go after their travel

Through Earth.

Oh my God,

I believe this life is

Where all the humans

Are asleep.

This life is a dream

And the afterlife is the reality,

Where all the dead awaken.

So, I know all the family members

Who have left this Earth,

And returned to their life

In Heaven,

To be with You,

All know the truth,

As they are all with

The Omnipotent,

The Omnipresent,

The Omniscient.

As they now see You

And they now hear You,

I pray with all my belief and faith

Not to cry,

Not to feel lonely,

And not to be sad

As they have returned home

To You.

My God,

The Omnipotent,

I pray for all the living creation

To believe and have faith in You,

And know

You are the beginning

And the end.

You give

And You take

All life back to You.

I pray we the living on Earth

Throughout this one life,

Know we are all on the same path

As we travel to You.

So, I shall be happy.

So, I shall be faithful.

So, I shall be hopeful

As I live this life for You.

I have faith and believe

Every soul that breathes,

And all that do not,

Are all on the same path,

The path to my God,

The Omnipotent.

As life through Earth

Is a day,

Everyone is greeted

By the Omnipotent

As we,

The creation,

On, above, and beyond Earth,

Will meet again

As we are all

TRAVELING THROUGH DUSK THROUGH DAWN.

So Be It

UNION AT DAWN

My God,

The Omnipotent,

Bless my heart

So, I can accept

All differences into my house

As You have created

Different races,

Different colors,

And different religions

In Your one home,

The universe.

Why then,

My God,

My Creator,

Do humans force

All to act the same?

Believe the same?

Even look the same?

You, my God, created

The mountains,

The seas,

And the lands.

You, my God, created

The rainbows,

The raindrops,

The scorching Sun's rays,

The flowers,

And the trees.

They all look different,

Yet they stand in their places

To serve all humans

Without asking about

Race, color, or religion.

The Sun pours sunlight,

The rain pours its blessings,

As does the pure clean breeze

That flows over

All race, color, and religion

Without any complaints.

Oh my God,

Then,

Why do we the creation

Seek to be powerful?

Why do we

The humans judge

All the differences?

My God,

Why do we not realize

We are not the Creator,

Nor are we the Judge?

Oh my God, my Creator,

Today,

I, Your creation,

Raise my hands

As I bow my head to You,

The Omnipotent,

The Omnipresent,

The Omniscient,

To accept all

Your creation as just that,

Your blessed creation.

May this darkness that

Has engulfed

Your humans to belong

In the same group,

Same house,

Same thoughts,

Not divide or falter

My faith in You,

The Omnipotent,

As I believe

You know what is right.

I am just a creation

Who shall not judge,

But be judged

By only You.

Oh my God,

I pray this dark night

Dividing all Your creation

Ends

As Your Sun rises.

With Your

Blessed fingers,

You say,

Be,

And You, my Lord, my Creator,

Break dawn open,

And finally

We the creation

At Your will

Shall be in

UNION AT DAWN.

So Be It

UNITEDLY WALK OUT OF DARKNESS INTO DAWN

Oh my God,

The Omnipotent,

I pray to You

On this day

For all

Your creation

Who are suffering

Today.

I see health issues.

I see financial crisis.

I see divisions between

Your creation.

Oh my God,

I pray for good health,

For good wealth,

And for united humans

With humanity.

Oh my God,

I pray the world

Leaves all alone

When they need space,

Yet be there

SPIRITUAL SONGS V: DAWN THROUGH DUSK

For each other,

Not against each other.

Oh my God,

Let the bad mouths

Of the evil voices

Of confusion,

Division,

And superiority

Not take away peace,

Faith,

And hope.

I pray to You,

Oh my God,

With all my being,

Allow all Your creation

To unite under

The blessed umbrella of knowledge

Of the Omnipotent,

The Omnipresent,

And the Omniscient,

And

For each other,

UNITEDLY WALK OUT OF DARKNESS INTO DAWN.

So Be It

ANN MARIE RUBY

WISDOM FROM DAWN

From dawn through dusk

Through dawn,

Oh my God,

I pray to You.

May my mind,

My body,

And my soul

Be free from all sadness,

Agitation,

Depression,

Worries,

Turbulences,

And anxieties.

May my mind,

My body,

And my soul

Never have distrust in God.

I know the devil prays for me to tremble,

To fall,

To be weak,

And to gain these attitudes.

I pray to You,

My God,

As You are the Healer,

And my sufferings are my medicine

Through which

I, the human, become stronger.

I pray

Through all my sufferings,

May I not be poisoned through

These attributes.

May You,

My God, my Creator,

Heal me

As I carry within my mind,

My body,

And my soul,

My blessed prayers.

Oh my God,

May my voice,

My words,

And the blessed sounds of prayers

Uttered from my lips

Be the prayer beads of

WISDOM FROM DAWN.

So Be It

YOUR NAME ON MY LIPS FROM DAWN

My God, my Creator,

The Omnipotent,

I pray on this day,

With my mind, body, and soul,

Let there be protection.

Let there be no harm,

Physical or spiritual,

As I give

My mind, body, and soul to You.

Through my faith, hope, and peace,

I have tied a blessed knot with You.

With this umbrella,

I know I am eternally

Under Your protection.

No evil can touch me

Nor harm me

As I have the umbrella of protection

From my God, my Creator,

Throughout eternity

With

YOUR NAME ON MY LIPS FROM DAWN.

So Be It

ABOUT THE AUTHOR

"Meet Ann Marie Ruby from Nashville, Tennessee.
This is her story."

Ann Marie Ruby was born into a diplomatic family for which she had the privilege of traveling the world. This upbringing made the whole world her one family. She never saw a country as a foreign country yet as a neighbor who was there for her as she would be there for them. After all, isn't that what families do for one another?

Ann Marie became an author as she started to place her chosen words into the pages of her diaries. She knew she must collect all her thoughts and produce them into different diaries. Each diary became her different books.

Ann Marie's life goal is not to just write something but only what she believes in. So all her thoughts and words remained within the pages of her diaries until she realized it was time she must share them with you. Otherwise, she felt selfish and knew that was not her characteristic as she lives for everyone, not just for herself.

INTERNATIONAL #1 BESTSELLING AUTHOR:

Ann Marie became an international number-one bestselling author of twenty-nine books. Alongside being a full-time author. She loves to write articles on her website where she can have a better connection with all of you. Ann Marie, a dream psychic, became a blogger and a humanitarian only because she believes in you and herself as a complete, honest, and open family.

PERSONAL:

Ann Marie is an American who grew up in Brisbane, Australia. She has resided all across the United States and is currently living in Nashville, Tennessee. In her spare time when she is not writing books, she loves to meditate, pray, listen to music, cook, and write blog posts.

BESTSELLING:

Ann Marie's books have placed her on top 100 bestselling charts in various countries including the Netherlands, United States, United Kingdom, Canada, and Germany. In 2020, she became a household name as her books began to consistently rank #1 on multiple bestselling charts. *The Netherlands: Land Of My Dreams* and *Everblooming: Through The Twelve Provinces Of The Netherlands*, both became overnight number-one bestsellers in the United States.

In 2020, *The Netherlands: Land Of My Dreams* also became a bestseller in the Netherlands and Canada, consistently becoming #1 on various lists and one of the top selling books on Amazon NL. *Everblooming: Through The Twelve Provinces Of The Netherlands* became #37 on the Netherlands top 100 bestselling Amazon books chart which includes all books from all genres. Ann Marie's other books have also made various top 100 bestselling lists and received multiple accolades including *Eternal Truth: The Tunnel Of Light* which was named as one of eight thought-provoking books by women.

ROMANCE FICTION:

Ann Marie's *Kasteel Vrederic* series was written in a diary fashion. She has always kept a diary herself, so she thought her characters too could keep a diary. All of their diaries became individual books yet collectively, they are a part of a family, the Kasteel Vrederic family.

OTHER BOOKS:

All of Ann Marie's nonfiction and fiction books are available globally. You can take a look at the titles at the end of this book.

THE NETHERLANDS:

Ann Marie revealed why many of her books revolve around the Netherlands, sharing that as a dream psychic, she had seen the historical past of a country in her dreams and was later able to place a name to the country. This is described in detail in *Spiritual Lighthouse: The Dream Diaries Of Ann Marie Ruby* and *The Netherlands: Land Of My Dreams* where she also wrote about her plans to eventually move to the Netherlands.

Ann Marie has received letters on behalf of His Majesty King Willem-Alexander and Her Majesty Queen Máxima of the Netherlands after they received her books *The Netherlands: Land Of My Dreams* and *Everblooming: Through The Twelve Provinces Of The Netherlands*. Additionally, Ann Marie has received letters on behalf of His Excellency Mark Rutte, the Prime Minister of the Netherlands for her books.

WRITING:

Ann Marie also is acclaimed globally as one of the top voices in the spiritual space, however, she is recognized for her writing abilities published across many genres namely spirituality, lifestyle, inspirational quotations, poetry, fiction, romance, history, travel, social awareness, and more. Her writing style is hailed by critics and readers alike as making readers feel as though they have made a friend.

FOLLOW THE AUTHOR:

Now as you have found her book, why don't you and Ann Marie become friends? Join her and become a part of her global family. Ann Marie shall always give you books which you will read and then find yourself as a part of her book family.

For more information about Ann Marie Ruby, any one of her books, or to read her blog posts and articles, subscribe to her website, www.annmarieruby.com.

Follow Ann Marie Ruby on Twitter, Facebook, Instagram, Threads, and Pinterest:

@TheAnnMarieRuby

BOOKS BY THE AUTHOR

INSPIRATIONAL QUOTATIONS:

1. *Spiritual Travelers: Life's Journey From The Past To The Present For The Future*
2. *Spiritual Messages: From A Bottle*
3. *Spiritual Journey: Life's Eternal Blessings*
4. *Spiritual Inspirations: Sacred Words Of Wisdom*
5. *Spiritual Ark: The Enchanted Journey Of Timeless Quotations*

SPIRITUAL SONGS SERIES:

1. *Spiritual Songs: Letters From My Chest*
2. *Spiritual Songs II: Blessings From A Sacred Soul*
3. *Spiritual Songs III: The Rising Lotus*
4. *Spiritual Songs IV: Dusk Through Dawn*
5. *Spiritual Songs V: Dawn Through Dusk*

KASTEEL VREDERIC SERIES:

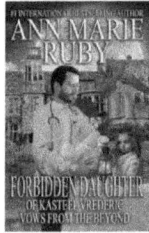

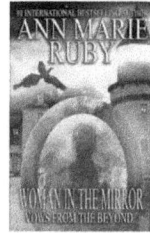

1. *Eternally Beloved: I Shall Never Let You Go*
2. *Evermore Beloved: I Shall Never Let You Go*
3. *Be My Destiny: Vows From The Beyond*
4. *Heart Beats Your Name: Vows From The Beyond*
5. *Entranced Beloved: I Shall Never Let You Go*
6. *Forbidden Daughter Of Kasteel Vrederic: Vows From The Beyond*
7. *The Immortality Serum: Vows From The Beyond*
8. *Woman In The Mirror: Vows From The Beyond*

Upcoming – *Bride Of The Immortal: Vows From The Beyond*

RELATED TO THE *KASTEEL VREDERIC* SERIES:

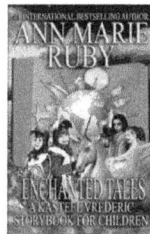

1. *Shattered Wings: Diary Of A Child Bride*

2. *The Bride, The Groom, And The Ghost*
3. *The Haunting Of MacNider Hospital*
4. *Enchanted Tales: A Kasteel Vrederic Storybook For Children*

Upcoming – *Brother Bear And The Four Investigators: A Kasteel Vrederic Storybook For Children*

NONFICTION:

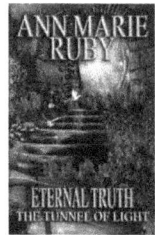

1. *Spiritual Lighthouse: The Dream Diaries Of Ann Marie Ruby*
2. *The World Hate Crisis: Through The Eyes Of A Dream Psychic*
3. *Eternal Truth: The Tunnel Of Light*

TRAVEL:

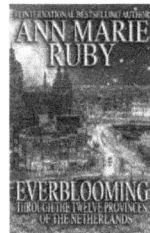

1. *The Netherlands: Land Of My Dreams*
2. *Everblooming: Through The Twelve Provinces Of The Netherlands*

POETRY:

1. *Love Letters: The Timeless Treasure*
2. *Melodies Of Humanity: The Golden Keys*

www.ingramcontent.com/pod-product-compliance
Lightning Source LLC
LaVergne TN
LVHW011221080426
835509LV00005B/252

9 7 9 8 9 9 1 7 4 1 6 8 2